HOOVER INSTITUTION STUDIES

Guerrillas in History

Guerrillas in History

Lewis H. Gann

Hoover Institution Press

Stanford University · Stanford, California

The Hoover Institution on War, Revolution and Peace, founded at Stanford University in 1919 by the late President Herbert Hoover, is a center for advanced study and research in public and international affairs in the twentieth century. The views expressed in its publications are entirely those of the authors and do not necessarily reflect the views of the Hoover Institution.

Hoover Institution Studies 28
© 1971 by the Board of Trustees of the Leland Stanford Junior University
All rights reserved
Library of Congress Catalog Card Number: 76-132819
Standard Book Number 8179-3281-x

Contents

Preface

A hundred years ago a mere handful of military experts in colonial armies were very much preoccupied with the problem of "small wars." Today, in a much wider context, guerrilla warfare has become a subject of popular debate. Many revolutionary intellectuals now look upon this type of action as the answer to all revolutionary problems, as a means of radicalizing the masses as well as a sure road to victory. Guerrilla warfare has acquired an aura of romance that once used to be reserved for the exploits of pioneers in the Wild West. The very fashions of many urban intellectuals—beards, boots, and all—have been influenced by the real or supposed examples of Cuban partisans. Yet guerrilla warfare is neither romantic nor new, nor has it always served a revolutionary cause. Neither is it a certain road to victory.

The present monograph is a revised and widely expanded version of a short paper entitled "Guerrillas and Insurgency," published in March 1966 in the *Military Review.* This study does not in any way pretend to be an exhaustive treatment of the subject, for a full account would fill many volumes and would cover the history of the whole world. The examples used are purely for purposes of illustration. Since the essay is primarily historical in nature, only passing reference is made to such current activities as the guerrilla movement in Angola, the attempts to conduct partisan war in the Congo, the clashes between Israelis and Arabs on the west bank of the Jordan River, or the present fighting in Viet Nam.

I am grateful to the editor of the *Military Review* for permitting me to use material previously published in his journal. I am indebted also to Colonel Clarence Clendenen, to Mr. Harold T. Ellis, to Colonel Leonard Humphreys, and to Mr. Janos Radvanyi for their comments. I should like to thank Mrs. Edna Halperin for her editing. Miss Mildred Teruya has provided further editorial assistance and has reread the manuscript; she and Mrs. Cassandra Butler have kindly done the typing.

L. H. Gann,
Senior Fellow, Hoover Institution

1. Partisan Warfare in the Preindustrial Age

"Small wars" are as old as human conflict. The Bible contains some splendid accounts of partisan operations such as the early struggles of the Maccabees. Historians of war, however, have perhaps paid too little attention to the activities of guerrilla fighters. It is usually easier to chronicle the clashes of great armies than to document scattered operations that lack the glamour of set battle pieces. Guerrilla operations moreover comprise a vast range of military actions that frequently overlap – colonial wars, social wars wages by one class against another, guerrilla wars between hostile tribes, or campaigns fought as an adjunct to major military operations, to name just a few.

These campaigns are difficult to categorize. They differ a good deal from one another, and there are also enormous variations from country to country, from century to century. Yet certain themes seem to recur through the ages. Judas Maccabaeus, the famed Jewish warrior of antiquity, would have had little to learn from Mao Tse-tung concerning the art of mounting guerrilla actions and expanding them into a national war. About 166 B.C., when the people of Judea were being ground under the heel of the hated Greco-Syrian conquerors, who tried both to Hellenize and despoil their subjects, Jewish militants mounted a series of small actions. The insurgents first of all hid "in secret places in the wilderness" where they lived "as wild animals do." They acquired great skill in making surprise attacks under cover of night, in suddenly striking at ships, harbors, and other installations, and at hitting the enemy while he was off balance. In time the insurgents extended their operations.

Judas Maccabaeus and they that were with him privately went into the towns: and calling together their kinsmen and friends, and taking unto them such as continued in the Jews' religion, they assembled six thousand men . . . So coming unawares upon the towns and cities. He set them on fire, and taking possession of the

1

most commodious places, he made no small slaughter of the enemy. And especially in the nights he went upon these expeditions, and the fame of his valour spread abroad everywhere.[1]

Judas seems to have made a special effort to secure support among the poor. His followers in time managed to seize well-fortified base areas, and his military operations became increasingly ambitious. "Moreover they slew above twenty thousand of them that were with Timotheus and Bacchides who fought against them, and they made themselves masters of the high strong-holds: and they divided amongst them many spoils, giving equal portions to the feeble, the fatherless and the widows, yea and the aged also." In the end Judas was able to wage a full-scale war. He won a number of major battles, turned Jerusalem into the center of his operations, engaged new priests, revived the observance of the Law, and at the end of 165 B.C. solemnly rededicated the Temple, the nation's religious and national sanctuary.

The problems of the Maccabees were similar in many ways to those of other national liberation leaders of later periods. Judea was a small, weak country, with its people dependent mainly on agriculture. Their "cities" were minor marketing centers whose inhabitants made their living as artisans, in small-scale trade, and—as often as not—in farming outside the town gates. From the military point of view, the Jews were deficient in both numbers and technology. The Syrians, for instance, used war elephants as "tanks," whereas the Maccabees could not afford this expensive equipment. Judas and his successors, however, were superior to the enemy in morale; they had a tightly knit religious and social organization and a burning faith. They fought for what they knew. They enjoyed wide popular support. They stood on their own ground against an enemy dependent on long and difficult lines of communication. The Jews were able to survive even devastating defeats by switching back to guerrilla warfare, and finally managed to consolidate their independence by a combination of diplomacy and competent military leadership.

Guerrilla warfare also comes easily to primitive nomadic

[1] 2 Macc. 8: 1-7.

peoples who lack the means to raise regular armies. The medieval Welsh, who were warlike, cattle-keeping hillsmen, waged bitter guerrilla wars against one another. Their skill at waging small wars stood them in good stead, too, during the Middle Ages when they had to do battle against Anglo-Norman invaders. The Welsh, in fact, were among the most outstanding practitioners of the art of partisan warfare. As Giraldus Cambrensis, a brilliant twelfth-century Welsh scholar, put it:

> This light armed people, relying more on their activity than on their strength, cannot struggle for the field of battle . . . [But] though defeated and put to flight one day, they are ready to resume the combat on the next, neither dejected by their loss nor their dishonour . . . they harass the enemy by embuscades and nightly sallies . . . Bold in the first onset, they cannot bear a repulse . . . [but] their courage manifests itself chiefly in retreat, when they frequently return, and, like the Parthians, shoot their arrows behind them . . . Neither oppressed by hunger or cold, nor fatigued by martial labours, nor despondent in adversity . . . they are as easy to overcome in a single battle, as difficult to subdue in a protracted war.[2]

The Welsh enjoyed in addition the unusual advantage of having developed a missile weapon of unusual power by the standards of the time. The Welsh longbow (soon to be adopted by English archers) was a deadly instrument of war that could pierce a knight's armor, and provided the Welsh guerrillas with exceptional firepower.

The English, however, gradually learned how to deal with their elusive enemies. Contemporary military thought found expression in the reflections of Giraldus Cambrensis concerning warfare in Wales. Giraldus stressed the need for correlating political with military action, for creating strong bases capable of methodically securing the country. Suitably equipped light forces wear out the enemy by sustained counterblows. The Welshmen's supplies would be cut and they would finally have to surrender. Giraldus Cambrensis's own words are worth quoting. His chapter on war in Wales is still a classic of counterguerrilla literature in history:

[2]Giraldus Cambrensis, *The Itinerary through Wales* and *The Description of Wales,* Introd. by W. Llewelyn Williams (London, J. M. Dent, 1908), pp. 192 and 193.

3

The prince who would wish to subdue this nation and govern it peaceably, must use this method . . . Let him divide their strength, and by bribes and promises endeavor to stir up one against the other . . . In the autumn let not only the marshes, but also the interior part of the country be strongly fortified with castles, provisions and confidential families. In the meantime the purchase of corn, cloth, and salt, with which they are usually supplied from England, should be strictly interdicted; and well-manned ships placed as a guard on the coast . . . Afterwards, when the severity of winter approaches . . . and the mountains no longer afford hope of pasturage . . . let a body of light-armed infantry penetrate into their woody and mountainous retreats, and let these troops be supported and relieved by others; and thus by frequent changes, and replacing the men who are either fatigued or slain in battle, this nation may be ultimately subdued.[3]

In the end, however, the Welshmen's skill at guerrilla warfare did not prevail against the hosts mobilized by feudal England. The invaders were economically superior to the Welsh and commanded greater military resources. The English held command of the sea. They methodically penetrated the country; they secured their conquests by stone castles. These strongholds could not easily be attacked by tribesmen who lacked the means to manufacture siege engines and who had no commissariat enabling them to sustain troops in the field over long periods. After a struggle lasting through several centuries, the military policy advocated by Giraldus Cambrensis proved successful, and Wales fell to the English invaders.

In medieval Wales partisans fought to safeguard their existing tribal constitution against invaders from abroad. From times immemorial, however, guerrilla warfare has also been used in class conflicts. Wars between the rich and the poor are probably as old as the institution of property itself. Aristotle's *Politics* has a great deal to say concerning class wars. So has the Bible. One of the most ancient recorded conspiracies of history centered on the Cave of Adullam, where David, the future king of Israel, hid from Saul, the reigning monarch. The Old Testament tersely describes the kind of people who joined David. "And every one that was in

[3]Giraldus Cambrensis, *Itinerary through Wales*, pp. 198-99.

4

distress, and every one that was in debt, and every one that was discontented, gathered themselves unto him; and he became a captain over them."[4]

Rural conspiracies of such a kind have taken many different forms throughout history, from Biblical to modern times. Where the terrain proved suitable, discontented peasants, debtors, or criminals might take to the mountains or forests. They would prey on noblemen and their bailiffs or on traveling merchants. They often professed a burning hatred of lawyers and moneylenders. They commonly claimed to help the poor against the rich; and provided outlaws left the peasantry alone, they could usually rely on help from the common people. Backward and inhospitable mountain regions of the kind found in nineteenth-century Sicily, Calabria, and Greece provided bandits with their traditional hunting grounds.[5] Highwaymen of the Robin Hood variety could also operate in countries with a relatively advanced agriculture, such as eighteenth-century England or Western Germany. In the Rhine-Main area, folk memories of Schinderhannes (Johann Bückler), a late eighteenth-century robber, live on to this day. Little children are still told stories of how Schinderhannes used to take cash from the wealthy and give alms to the poor (a pious legend that had little basis in fact).

Rural unrest, however, could take much more serious forms than "social banditry." The history of preindustrial Europe is punctuated with peasant rebellions. These differed in scope and intensity, from ferocious jacqueries—spontaneous outbreaks without specific long-term goals—to great insurgencies that shook society to its foundations. But however violent, these risings had serious limitations. No European peasant-army ever managed to overthrow an entire feudal state. At best, embattled farmers succeeded, like the leaders of the Swiss *Urkantone*, in freeing some inaccessible mountain area from foreign rule.

The reasons for the lack of any notable degree of success

[4]1 Sam.: 22, 1.

[5]For the standard work, see Eric J. Hobsbawm, *Primitive Rebels: Studies in Archaic Forms of Social Movements in the 19th and 20th Centuries* (Manchester University Press, 1959).

in any of these peasant risings did not necessarily reflect a weakness in military technology. Even as early as the later Middle Ages, tacticians in various European countries had begun to solve the problem of how to beat the poorly disciplined armored knight with his cumbersome and expensive equipment, the feudal warrior par excellence. English archers, having adopted the longbow from Welsh tribesmen, learned how to sustain a rapid rate of fire and how to pierce the horseman's armor. Swiss pikemen massed in solid phalanges presented a terrible threat to armored horsemen. Czech Hussites trained to wheel wagons in solid squares and thereby also solved the problem of beating the knight on his own ground.[6]

The European peasant hosts, however, suffered from weaknesses that went beyond those of a purely military, and even those of an ideological, kind. For an example, we shall take the German Peasants' War (1524-25), one of many similar risings. In this upheaval, the greatest revolutionary movement in German history, the peasants put forward clearly framed programs for the abolition of villein service, the reduction of tithes and rents, the relief of debts, and the institution of rural self-government. The rebellious peasants were far from unsophisticated. Many insurgents had seen military service as *Landsknechte* or mercenaries; they were well supplied with pikes and arquebuses; they even secured plentiful supplies of artillery.[7] Many peasant leaders had some education. Indeed the main impetus seems to have come from the wealthier farmers, from innkeepers, smiths, waggoners, and rural officials, rather than from the very poor. (This pattern of leadership was equally common during other periods and in other parts of the world, such as the Iberian Peninsula or Eastern Europe, where country-bred insurgents would often select their chiefs from the ranks of the impoverished minor gentry, the better-off farmers, or the rural clergy.) The German rebels, too, like many others of their kind, managed to secure allies among other social

[6]Hans Delbrück, *Geschichte der Kriegskunst* . . . (Berlin, Walter de Gruyter Verlag, 1964), Vols. 3 and 4 *passim.*

[7]Günther Franz, *Der deutsche Bauernkrieg,* 2 vols. (Munich and Berlin, R. Oldenbourg, 1933-35), *passim.*

classes, especially the mine-workers, and also impoverished rural craftsmen and "evangelical" intellectuals.

The peasants, however, could not overcome certain fundamental weaknesses. Their main problem was lack of leadership, of trained cadres, and of adequate discipline. Even when victorious in battle, rural insurgents could not easily consolidate their gains. The peasants suffered also from severe regional divisions aggravated by lack of communications. (In Germany, for instance, the Bavarian peasants refused to join the rising; most of the more backward North likewise stood aloof.) The rebels moreover differed in their programs. In addition their armed forces had trouble in remaining active over long periods of time, for their fields needed attention and work on the farm required a great deal of manpower. (Even in the Boer War, at the beginning of the present century, Boers would often leave their units for varying periods to look after their farms.)

Rebellious peasants moreover faced formidable political difficulties. Farmers were ill equipped to run the machinery of a centralized state, especially at a time when even neighboring village communities often failed to see eye to eye on common problems. The rebels, often enough, looked to the past, and called for the restoration of real or imagined customs of bygone days. The peasants frequently supposed monarchs to be friendly to their cause, and commonly called for no more than the removal of "wicked" councillors from the entourage of the prince, a program that bore little relevance to political realities.

The weaknesses and the strengths of peasant insurrectionaries become apparent by reference to Ireland, where class divisions became further complicated by those of a religious and ethnic kind. In Ireland, English and Scottish settlers professing the Protestant faith clashed with the indigenous Catholic peasantry and gentry. Immigrants and natives battled for land, power, and social position, with the indigenous population coming out second-best. (The problems of seventeenth-century – and to some extent also eighteenth-century – Ireland in some ways curiously presaged those of twentieth-century Kenya, where native peasants fought against European landowners in defense of the natives' ancient, or reputedly ancient, way of life.) The

Irish made formidable guerrilla fighters. Their island, with its inhospitable bog and hilly country, provided innumerable hiding places to guerrilla gangs. Ireland moreover was a poverty-stricken land. Irishmen, like Scotsmen, Swiss, and Castilians, dwelt in backward parts of Europe whose resources were inadequate to satisfy the ambitions of the more enterprising peasants. Hence Scottish and Swiss mountaineers, like Irishmen, would often seek employment as mercenaries abroad. The Irish were skilled in partisan fighting. This is how Macaulay with his inimitable prose describes the tactics of the elusive "Rapparees," the native Catholic resistance fighters, who continued the struggle against the English after the regular Irish armies had been beaten by the end of the seventeenth century:

> The English complained that it was no easy matter to catch a Rapparee. Sometimes, when he saw danger approaching, he lay down in the long grass of the bog, and then it was as difficult to find him as to find a hare sitting. Sometimes he sprang into a stream, and lay there, like an otter, with only his mouth and nostrils above the water. Nay, a whole gang of banditti would, in the twinkling of an eye, transform itself into a crowd of harmless labourers. Every man took his gun to pieces, hid the lock in his clothes, stuck a cork in the muzzle, stopped the touch hole with a quill, and threw the weapon into the next pond. Nothing was to be seen but a train of poor rustics, who had not so much as a cudgel among them, and whose humble look and crouching walk seemed to show that their spirit was thoroughly broken to slavery. When the peril was over, when the signal was given, every man flew to the place where he had hid his arms, and soon the robbers were in full march towards some Protestant mansion.[8]

Ireland, however, like ancient Wales, was exposed to the pressure of the invaders' sea power. By and large, British warships managed to insulate the Irish resistance movement from continental, especially from French, supporters, even though a few foreign units did occasionally manage to land on Irish soil. Because Ireland was geographically close to England, British troops could easily be reinforced from home. The supporters of the "Ascendancy" knew the

[8]Thomas Babington Macaulay, *The History of England from the Accession of James II* (Chicago, Bedford and Clarke, 1888), IV, 175.

country's terrain just as well as did their subjects. Nor did the Irish climate hold any terrors for Englishmen and Scotsmen. The British rulers were therefore able to build up a fairly efficient system of control. This hold was shaken for a time during the American Revolution, when the British had to make many concessions to the local Protestants; but never again did Irish nationalists succeed in challenging British power until the twentieth century.

In Eastern Europe, the classical region of guerrilla warfare, peasant risings were perhaps even more common, partly perhaps for topographical reasons, partly because clashes between social strata were intensified by overlying religious and ethnic tensions. The history of Eastern Europe is mirrored by its peasant revolts. Particularly noteworthy were the Hungarian peasant insurrection of 1514, led by George Dósza, a Szekler nobleman; a great Croatian rising initiated in 1573 by Matija Gubéc, a peasant from the hills of central Croatia; and the Transsylvanian revolt of 1784, supported mainly by Rumanian peasants and miners, directed by Nicolae Horia, a well-to-do farmer. Another great Eastern European peasant insurrectionary was Yemelyan Ivanovich Pugachev (1726-75), an outstanding Cossack leader. Pugachev proclaimed himself "Tsar" Peter III. He promised to drive out his "wicked wife" Catherine and her evil advisers and to liberate the serfs. Pugachev attracted wide popular support; but after bitter and bloody fighting his rising, like the German Peasants' Revolt, was crushed with great slaughter.

The European peasant revolts of the seventeenth and eighteenth century were paralleled, on a smaller scale, by outbreaks among black slaves in the New World. In countries as far afield as Brazil and Jamaica, runaway bondsmen battled against their masters. Some of these fugitives set up independent little commonwealths in remote bush and mountain country. In Brazil, black men seeking freedom established their own settlements known as *quilombos*, where Africans attempted to recreate their own societies on American soil. The most important of these communities was the "Negro Republic" of Palmares in Pernambuco, which maintained its independence throughout most of the seventeenth century. After bitter fighting, the state of Palmares was wiped out in 1694. Its destruction probably marked a milestone in Brazilian history. Had Palmares continued to exist, the Portuguese might well have been confined to the coast, facing not one but several independent black states in the interior.[9]

The history of Negro guerrilla warfare in the New World still remains to be written. Black revolutionary outbreaks ranged all the way from minor skirmishing in the Jamaican backwoods to a country-wide slave rising in Haiti at the beginning of the nineteenth century. This rising we shall discuss later. African rebels could sometimes make headway where the terrain was exceptionally favorable to guerrillas, or where the country proved insalubrious to white soldiers at a time when Europeans had no effective remedies against malaria and yellow fever. In addition, the numerical proportion between whites and blacks played a decisive role. North America, for instance, never experienced insurrections on the Brazilian or Caribbean scale because the blacks were too few and the whites too many.

The long-term effects of all these rural risings, whether white or black, are not easy to assess. In the Balkans, the possibility of Christian resistance may have imposed some practical checks on the exactions of Muslim tax-gatherers and landowners. The Ottomans could never fully control the more remote and inaccessible regions of the Balkan Peninsula, where Christian rebel leaders kept alive the flame of resistance. Balkan insurgents thus helped to shape the ethnic consciousness of subject nationalities like the Rumanians and the Serbs. Serbian nationalism, for instance, gained a tremendous boost from the exploits performed by the *hajduci*, the guerrilla leaders in the mountains, half bandit, half freedom fighter. The Rumanians derived inspiration from Horia's insurrection. The memory of peasant revolts may also have contributed to the creation of a more modern class consciousness. (Before the First World War, for instance, Agrarian Socialists in Hungary thus proposed to unveil a statue to Dósza, who was represented by conventional textbooks as a bloodthirsty robber.)

In the New World, black resistance presumably helped to impose certain customary restrictions on slavery in regions

[9] Raymond R. Kent, "Palmares, An African State in Brazil," *Journal of African History*, vol. 6, no. 2 (1965): 161-75.

where the terrain favored the rebels, and where the population ratio between whites and blacks offered some advantage to African resistance leaders. In Jamaica, for instance, the so-called maroons succeeded in maintaining a recognized form of home rule over remote villages situated in the far interior where British troops could not effectively counter guerrilla tactics. In certain countries, especially in Brazil, the military cost of repression also supplied opponents of slavery with financial arguments, in addition to those put forward for religious, humanitarian, and social reasons.

Throughout the seventeenth and eighteenth centuries, the effects of all these risings were nevertheless limited. The insurgents usually had no recourse other than guerrilla actions. Their risings were of a local kind. Their victories were confined to the backwoods. No slave insurrection ever endangered the Spanish or the Portuguese empire in the New World as a whole. Irish peasants could not destroy the Protestant Ascendancy. Balkan guerrillas could not liquidate Muslim rule in Europe. The power-differential between peasant insurrectionaries and incumbent power-holders was simply too overwhelming to permit of permanent revolutionary successes.

Rural guerrilla warfare did, however, exert some influence on conventional fighting between legitimate princes. Where their dynastic interests were at stake, the crowned heads of Europe were not united by any kind of class solidarity. Few monarchs scrupled to make use of popular insurgents to incommode hostile prince. A widespread misconception pictures the eighteenth century as an era of limited wars. In those supposedly happier days, rulers were said to have fought according to certain fixed rules that prevented treachery. The common people, according to this school of thought, were not expected to participate, and civilians were spared the horrors of war. In Churchill's sonorous prose:

> No hatred, apart from military antagonism, was countenanced among the troops. All was governed by strict rules of war, into which bad temper was not often permitted to enter. The main acceptances of a polite civilization still reigned along the lines of opposing armies, and mob violence and mechanical propaganda

11

had not yet been admitted to the adjustment of international disputes.[10]

There is only some degree of truth in Churchill's generalizations. The field commanders of the eighteenth century formed a military internationale bound by a common code of courtesy; and the armies of this era consisted largely, though by no means entirely, of professional soldiers. Fortresses often imposed severe obstacles on mobility. Armies depended for their provisions on magazines. Road transport was poor. Supplies could most easily be carried by barges along rivers and canals. Supply services were generally inadequate. Much of the work that would in our days be entrusted to staff officers depended then on the private enterprise of commissaries and "court factors." Nevertheless, historians have tended to overemphasize the supposedly moderate, limited, and aristocratic nature of warfare in prerevolutionary Europe.

There was certainly some continuity between the military methods of the nineteenth century and those of preceding eras. The *levée en masse,* the appointment of bourgeois officers, the employment of unconventional and ruthless methods of warfare, the use of guerrillas as an adjunct to regular operations were by no means unfamiliar to the contemporaries of Gustavus Vasa of Sweden or Frederick the Great of Prussia.

Long before the age of the Jacobins, Sweden, during the Thirty Years' War, for instance, raised something like a national army. By 1630 King Gustavus Adolphus had mobilized a larger percentage of his country's population than Prussia managed to raise during the War of Liberation against Napoleon nearly two centuries later. Sweden's record was unusual but not exceptional. The Prussian army in 1740 accounted for a larger percentage of the country's civilian population than did the French army, based on the levée en masse in 1793.[11]

[10]Winston S. Churchill, *Marlborough: His Life and Times* (London, George G. Harrap and Co., 1934), II, 38.

[11]For these and other relevant figures, see, for instance, Freiherr H. F. P. von Freytag-Loringhoven, *Die Psyche der Heere* (Berlin, Mittler und Sohn, 1923), pp. 111-12; and Delbrück, *Geschichte der Kriegskunst,* IV, 200.

The armies were not officered solely by aristocrats. Many commoners, for instance, held important positions in the officer corps of Louis XIV. Historians tell of a swineherd who became a cornet, and of a rich printer's son who received a French marshal's baton during the reign of the "Sun King." Indeed the concept of *la carrière ouverte aux talents*, like so many other revolutionary ideals, owed a great deal to prerevolutionary practice.[12] Commanders of the age of elegance, whether of bourgeois or of aristocratic origin, were equally capable of acting in as ruthless and unscrupulous a fashion as any of their successors in subsequent ages.

The annals of the eighteenth century are also full of unprovoked conflicts and unsuspected assaults, made without the customary declaration of war.[13] Eighteenth-century generals would likewise plan coups that differed in no way

[12]The ability of military castes to fuse into a cohesive group persons derived from many different social strata and national origins deserves further investigation. It is worth mentioning here that even in socially conservative armies during a subsequent "Age of Reaction," supposedly aristocratic generals often traced their ancestry to men of humble stock. For instance, the Austrian army that marched against the Prussians in 1866 was led by Ludwig Ritter von Benedek, the son of a Hungarian doctor; Gideon Ritter von Krismanić was the son of a poor Croatian captain; and Alfred Freiherr von Henikstein, the grandson of a Jewish trader. See, for details, Gordon A. Craig, *The Battle of Königgrätz: Prussia's Victory over Austria, 1866* (Philadelphia, J. B. Lippincott, 1964); and Heinrich Friedjung, *Der Kampf um die Vorherrschaft in Deutschland 1859 bis 1866,* 2 vols. (Berlin, J. G. Cotta, 1912). It would be interesting to compare the social origins of guerrilla leaders with those of contemporary regular soldiers.

[13]In 1833 the Intelligence Branch of the British Quartermaster General's Department issued a study called *Hostilities Without Declaration of War: An Historical Abstract of the Cases in Which Hostilities Have Occurred Between Civilized Powers Prior to Declaration of War or Warning. . . .* (London, H. M. Stationery Office). Colonel J. F. Maurice, the compiler of this treatise, listed no fewer than 107 cases during the period 1700 to 1870 alone in which hostilities were commenced by subjects of European powers or of the United States without declaration of war. The author did not bother to mention any hostilities between Europeans and non-European peoples; otherwise his list would have been even vaster. Even as it is, the monograph makes an impressive showing. No European power ever allowed itself to be wholly restrained by the customs and usages of war. Many, in fact, sought to gain a sudden advantage by attacking their neighbors without warning, and many made use of irregular operations by sea or land in order to achieve their aims.

from special operations that have marked warfare from time immemorial. For instance, when the Elector of Bavaria decided to join the French against Austria during the War of the Spanish Succession (1701-14), his high command began the war in a fashion considered treacherous even by the standards of the least squeamish. Some fifty Bavarian officers disguised themselves as peasants bringing vegetables to the market-gate of the strategic city of Ulm. Suddenly they overpowered the sentries, and then admitted Bavarian troops into the defenseless city.

Eighteenth-century wars could moreover be extremely destructive. Belligerents would engage mounted irregulars, such as the Pandours in the Austrian and the Cossacks in the Russian service, whose conduct had become a byword for cruelty and rapine. Thus Prussia's losses in wealth and blood were in all likelihood proportionately much greater during the Seven Years' War (1756-63) than the whole of Germany's during the First or the Second World War. Beyond the Atlantic, eighteenth-century Frenchmen and Britons would also call on Red Indian guerrillas to carry death and destruction into the lands of their enemies. Whole regions would be devastated. The Palatinate and Bavaria suffered terrible ravages during the wars of Louis XIV.

Above all, rulers would endeavor to stir up malcontents against the rule of hostile princes. The French thus traditionally supported Jacobite clansmen in the Scottish Highlands against the Hanoverian kings of England. The Court of Versailles would sustain Hungarian rebels against the House of Austria. During the War of the Spanish Succession Ferenc Rákóczy II, the scion of a famous Transylvanian family, led a great rebellion against the Habsburgs, supported by money from the purse of Louis XIV, who did not disdain to support Rácóczy's peasant guerrillas. The enemies of France resorted to a similar strategy. England and Holland, for instance, welcomed outbreaks of the Huguenot peasantry in the Cévennes that led to a bloody guerrilla war. The rebellious Camisards (so-called from the white shirts that were their only uniform) performed prodigies of courage and savagery — inspired as they were by an apocalyptic creed of redemption. It was only with great difficulty that French troops supported by Catholic peasant militias put down the rising.

From the Great Powers' point of view, support for such risings nevertheless only served a subsidiary purpose. Established governments were quick enough to abandon their allies whenever the winds of fortune changed, and the guerrillas never won on their own.

Peasant resistance of the traditional kind proved equally ineffectual when it was directed against the social and political forces that produced the French Revolution and the Empire of Napoleon. The causes of the great revolution were complex. There were the thwarted social and economic ambitions of an important section of the French middle class. There was a misguided initial attempt on the part of the privileged orders to strengthen their positions against both the king and the mass of the people. There was peasant unrest, and bitter discontent among the poor provoked by an economic crisis. There was the weakness of an antiquated state machinery, and the inefficiency and the discriminatory nature of the tax system — to mention only some of the weaknesses besetting France.

But equally important was the fact that many troops became unreliable, since a large percentage of the common soldiers were drawn from the urban poor and often sympathized with the rebels. The higher nobility had relinquished many of the command posts in the army, and much of the actual leadership lay in the hands of indigent provincial nobles or even of bourgeois officers. The new French revolutionary armies, like the Swedish armies of the seventeenth century, rested on partial conscription. The Revolution appealed also to patriotic fervor. Warfare was influenced, too, by technical change. Firearms could now be manufactured with relative ease. Large numbers of troops could be moved to the battlefield and could be supplied on distant campaigns. Most important of all, the upkeep of a Napoleonic soldier was appreciably cheaper than that of an eighteenth-century mercenary. The new tactics of skirmishing and charging in columns could be taught more easily than the rigid linear tactics of old: hence the revolutionary armies at first enjoyed many advantages over their foreign enemies.

The policy of conscription, like French religious policies and many other aspects of the revolutionary state, proved bitterly unpopular, however, in many parts of the French

15

countryside. The French, fighting under the Tricolor, claimed to represent the cause of the "people." Yet, by a strange irony of history, the French revolutionary government, with its control over the regular forces, found itself in conflict with numerous partisan movements. Guerrilla war of the popular kind was usually waged against rather than for the Revolution. In 1793 the peasants of the Vendée unsuccessfully rose against the bourgeois Republic. So-called "brigandage" continued in the Vendée until the downfall of Napoleon despite, and perhaps even because of, the savage reprisals taken against the insurgents. During the Napoleonic era, in 1809, guerrillas also harried the French and their Bavarian allies in the Tyrol. In Belgium the Catholicism of the farm population was outraged. Sometimes, as in southern Italy, what seemed to be a religious movement, an outburst of rural fanaticism or superstition, carried with it a well-grounded and valid social protest, based on the belief that the revolutionary intellectuals of the south Italian cities neither knew nor cared about the real needs of the rural masses.[14]

The peasant-bred sharpshooters of the Tyrol and the Vendée all operated in what might be called backward and inaccessible "islands" situated within relatively advanced Western countries. Neither the Tyroleans nor the people of the Vendée were able to make any headway against modern armies. At the beginning of the nineteenth century, however, guerrilla warfare did become a factor of decisive importance in parts of what might be called the backward circumference of the Western world, in countries as far afield as Spain and Haiti, Serbia and Greece. Here country-born partisans, strengthened sooner or later by semi-regular or regular forces, managed to defeat conventional forces, with far-reaching consequences for the future.

The best-known case is that of Spain. The Iberian Peninsula has always been tough campaigning country. In the War of the Spanish Succession, operations on the Peninsula had commonly amounted to

> a war of petty armies, occasionally fighting small, fierce battles and making long marches about an enormous country in the main

[14] R. R. Palmer, *The Age of Democratic Revolution: A Political History of Europe and America, 1760-1800: The Struggle* (Princeton University Press, 1964), p. 21.

stony and desolate, . . . The sympathies of the countryside, however, played a serious part in the fortunes of the wandering armies, and a surge of national feeling was almost immediately decisive.[15]

A century later, when Napoleon's troops invaded the country, the Spaniards again showed their mettle. In Spain, unlike Russia or Prussia or many of the Austrian Crown lands, there was no serfdom. The Spanish guerrillas regarded the French as foreign intruders and as atheists to boot. The Spaniards were attached to the Catholic Church, whose creed was not challenged by the poor and whose monastic orders seemed to embody profound principles of social justice. The guerrilla forces remained loyal to the monarchy, and the British skillfully "nursed" the Spanish partisan movement. London sent advisers, arms, and ammunition; and British military operations on the Peninsula were themselves indispensable to the Spanish cause. The Spanish partisans blocked roads, raided lonely posts, captured couriers, and managed to cut off isolated French garrisons. The Spaniards also undertook larger operations, engaged regular forces two or three battalions strong, and cleared large areas of the enemy. The distinction between the front and the rear became blurred; so did the borderline between irregular and regular operations. Whenever the guerrillas felt strong enough, they fought a regular war. The Spaniards ably utilized the difficult nature of their local terrain. They pounced on the enemy's lines of communication and by their intervention managed to pin down something like twice their own numbers.[16]

The French, for their part, suffered from numerous weaknesses. They were unable to win over the Spanish people to their cause. They operated in a country where, as the saying went, small armies would be beaten and large armies would starve. Their leaders had been trained to conduct swift, audacious operations, to live off the country, and to pursue the enemy, even at the cost of security. But in Spain the Frenchmen's aggressive strategy would not work. Supplies were difficult to requisition in a poverty-stricken country. The partisans would attack the neglected flanks and

[15] Churchill, *Marlborough*, III,55.

[16] Otto Heilbrunn, *Warfare in the Enemy's Rear* (London, George Allen and Unwin, 1963), pp. 21-22.

17

rear of invading columns. Stragglers and foraging parties were cut down by enraged peasants driven to desperation by the depredations of the foreign soldiery. Above all, the Spanish guerrillas were supported by Wellington's British expeditionary force, the finest professional army in Europe. The Hispano-British effort created a constant drain on the military and financial resources of France. Napoleon was forced to disperse large forces in a wasteful war, troops that might have been used to better advantage in Central Europe. In the end, the British and Spaniards drove the French from the entire Iberian Peninsula, and thereby helped to topple the emperor from his throne.

Even more spectacular in some respects was the victory of the Haitian slaves over the French. Whereas in earlier ages Irish, Rumanian, or German serfs had vainly struggled for liberty against their lords, the black people of Haiti managed to overthrow completely the French ascendancy in their country, and to crush slavery as a local institution. The Haitians owed their success to an exceptional combination of circumstances. In the first place the French Revolution had shattered the cohesion of the French Establishment. The white population in Haiti first set an example of illegality, and in their struggle for mastery called for aid from free men of color. Finally the slaves themselves took to arms, and French rule gradually disintegrated. Not only were the local French divided into several factions, but the metropolitan country was itself surrounded by enemies and torn by revolution. The French forces in Haiti moreover depended for supplies and reinforcements on a country situated on the other side of the Atlantic. The black rebels had both extensive local backing and the advantage of numbers. They could rely on brilliant leaders, especially Toussaint L'Ouverture and Jacques Dessalines. Both the climate and the terrain favored the insurgents, for European soldiers, having no safeguard against tropical disease, died by the thousands. The Haitians made good use of both their vast numerical superiority and their knowledge of the countryside. They combined skillful concealment with sudden massive shock-assaults that finally laid low the weakened French forces.[17]

[17] C. L. R. James, *The Black Jacobins: Toussaint L'Ouverture and the San Domingo Revolution* (New York, Vintage Books, 1963), *passim*.

18

The rebels smashed slavery, expelled the British and later the French. They finally massacred or drove out the white population of Haiti as well as many mulattos, who occupied a desperate intermediate position between white lords and their black bondsmen.

In 1804 Haiti declared its independence. The black insurgents thus managed to free their country without drawing on the help of a regular army from abroad. But they could not, for a time, create a viable state, and for many years to come the country struggled along in a state of semi-anarchy interrupted by spells of tyranny.

In Serbia, the insurrectionary forces operated in different circumstances. The rebels were Christians; the incumbent authorities stood for Islam. The insurgents battled, not against a great military power, but against a decaying empire which, by the early nineteenth century, had become but a shadow of its former self. The Serbian rising, ironically enough, broke out at the time when the Ottoman monarchy was attempting to carry out a number of internal reforms in Serbia. But the Turkish ruling class, like the dominant French strata in Haiti, suffered from bitter internal dissensions, and the Serbs grasped a heaven-sent opportunity when the Janissaries, insubordinate Muslim mercenaries quartered upon the land, began to quarrel with their sovereign. The Janissaries first clashed with Hadji Mustafa, the Serbophile Turkish governor of Belgrade. Mustafa was murdered by insubordinate military chiefs, and in 1804 the Serbs took to arms, initially professing loyalty to the Sublime Porte. (In Haiti, also, some of the early black insurgents hoisted the white flag and called themselves *les Gens du Roi* — even though they had nothing in common with French legitimists.) In time, however, the breach between Christian and Muslim became irreparable. In 1815 the little Serbian peasant commonwealth secured a limited form of autonomy and a measure of international recognition. Later the Serbs gained additional concessions. These in turn helped to inspire other Christian risings against the Ottomans in Europe.

The Greek War of Independence against the Turks (1821-29) was a rising of an even more spectacular kind, in that the rebels fought on sea as well as on land. The Greek insurgents, like their counterparts in Serbia and Spain, were

19

men from different social classes. Greek merchants, peasants, clergymen, and seamen all took to arms. The struggle was waged with a ferocity that equaled the savagery of the wars in Spain, Serbia, and Haiti. The Greeks, like the Serbs and Spaniards, made good use of their mountainous terrain. They pounced on the Ottomans' excessively long lines of communication. The conflict at the same time became one of opposing nationalities, as Greeks and Turks frequently resorted to a strategy of mutual extermination.

From a historical standpoint, the war has a special interest in that the Greeks combined guerrilla warfare by land, of the kind familiar to all Balkan mountaineers, with a *guerre de course*, the naval equivalent of partisan warfare. (The navies of the world still depended on wind- rather than steam-power.) Greek merchant vessels were well armed to protect their cargoes against Barbary pirates and rovers of their own kith. Greek fishermen and sailors all knew how to fight. The Greek islands had indeed for long furnished most of the sailors in the Ottoman marine. The Turks found themselves unable to enlist adequate numbers of seaworthy recruits when their Greek subjects took to arms. The insurgents, for their part, taking full advantage of the deeply indented Greek shoreline, employed sea power to its best advantage. Since roads in those days were few and were often open to maritime assaults, commanders could not easily transport supplies by land. Hence command of the sea became a vital factor in the insurrection.

The Greek naval guerrillas displayed the same strengths and weaknesses as their brethren on land. They were capable of performing the most daring coups that ranged from minor naval engagements to acts of outright piracy. But Greek captains would often sail home when they felt like it. The crews suffered from indiscipline; and the navy, like the land forces, was torn by fierce faction fights. In spite of these shortcomings the Greeks retained command of the sea until Mehemet Ali, the pasha of Egypt, threw his well-drilled army and his fleet against the insurgents. The Greeks could not have prevailed against the combined Turko-Egyptian attacks but for the intervention of Great Britain, France, and Russia, whose naval forces destroyed the Muslim fleet at Navarino (1827), while the Ottoman Empire subsequently had to resist a Russian assault by land. The Greek guerrillas nevertheless had played a vital part in the liberation of their country. The Greek effort at sea moreover went beyond anything anticipated by Clausewitz, who had given inadequate attention to the impact of naval power on warfare.

The Greek maritime ventures, comparable in many ways to the exploits of Sir Francis Drake and of the Dutch "Sea Beggars" against Spain in the sixteenth century, stood out as the last important examples of popular guerrilla warfare at sea. Their feats could never again be repeated on a great scale in the subsequent age of armor-clad steamships, heavy guns, and the telegraph serviced by trained and salaried specialists. The Greeks, like the Haitians, were moreover unable to create a disciplined national army during their rising. Their administration for long remained in disarray. The final salvation of Greece only came from the European powers, and for a long time afterward the clan and faction fights of the war still continued to beset the new kingdom in peacetime.

At first sight these various risings seem to have nothing in common. The rebels, for instance, cannot be categorized simply as "progressive" or "reactionary." The Greeks were idealized by European intellectuals, who imagined that Epirote shepherds and Cretan sailors resembled heroes of antiquity like Themistocles and Leonidas. In Spain, on the other hand, the people rose to support what to many European intellectuals was a reactionary cause. The Spanish guerrillas fought for their own legitimate dynasty against the Napoleonic conquerors, against men whom the Spaniards regarded as impious aliens. The guerrillas of the Vendée battled against the principles of the French Revolution in defense of the Bourbon dynasty. The followers of Andreas Hofer, a Tyrolean guerrilla chief, struggled against Napoleonic troops in order to sustain the Habsburgs. All these rebels regarded themselves as loyal sons of the Catholic Church; they detested the social innovations brought about by intruders whom they considered to be no better than atheists. The Serbs and Greeks likewise drew some of their strength from religious traditions. The Haitians, on the other hand, were much more divided: some were Catholics, some were animists, and others professed syncretic creeds in which

21

Christianity strangely mingled with magic. Color played no part in the European struggles. In Haiti the combatants were divided into rigid color-castes that fixed hereditary status much more effectively than any form of feudalism had ever done in Europe. There were also military differences between the various risings. The Spaniards relied on help from a British expeditionary force, one of the best-led and best-trained regular armies in the world. The Greeks were a maritime people; even the Haitians made some use of sea power. The Serbian struggle was confined to the land. The Haitians above all relied on their own strength; the Greeks were saved finally by the intervention of the British, French, and Russian navies.

But there were also certain parallels in these struggles. They were all fought with extreme savagery. The insurgents always drew their main, though by no means their sole, strength from the villages. They all relied on mass support. They dwelt in relatively poor countries; they were hardy folk inured to hardships of many kinds; they found unity through a common hatred of a foreign ruler. They enunciated national aspirations and hearkened back to the glories of a real or imagined past. (Even black rebels of Haiti thus adopted an ancient Indian name for their island in order to give historical legitimacy to their new republic.) The Haitians, the Serbs, and the Greeks — though not the Spaniards — moreover fought against rulers who were divided amongst themselves and who lacked internal cohesion.

The military methods used by the guerrillas likewise displayed certain uniform features. When Clausewitz, the greatest military theoretician of the nineteenth century, analyzed the conditions required for successful guerrilla warfare, he came to conclusions that were similar in many ways to those reached by Giraldus Cambrensis in the early Middle Ages.[18] Clausewitz stressed that guerrilla warfare should be carried out in the interior of the country, that the theater of war should be extensive, that the country should be hard to traverse and difficult of access. Giraldus had

[18] Karl von Clausewitz, *On War,* trans. J. J. Graham, new and rev. ed. with an introduction and notes by F. N. Maude (London, Kegan Paul, Trench, Trubner and Co., 1940), III,341-50. (This classic chapter, Chap. XVI, Bk. 6, is entitled "Arming the Nation.")

enlarged upon the harsh environment of Wales, on its inhospitable mountains and forlorn swampland where "in time of peace, the young men, by penetrating the deep recesses of the woods and climbing the tops of mountains, learn by practice to endure fatigue."[19] Clausewitz argued that guerrilla war, while strategically on the defensive, should always seize the tactical initiative. Resolute leadership could kindle the flame of popular war and gradually blow it into a consuming flame. According to Clausewitz, partisans should never stake the success of their campaign on the outcome of a single battle. Giraldus likewise emphasized the advantages which protracted warfare offered to Welsh mountaineers.

There were other parallels between the two writers. Clausewitz, reacting against mechanical interpretations of warfare, stressed the supreme importance of morale and of a resolute material character. Giraldus (who was partly Welsh by origin) had boasted that in Wales "nobles as well as privates are instructed in the use of arms." Clausewitz, schooled in the doctrines of Kantian philosophy, pondered on the motives that would make men fight for freedom. Giraldus had contrasted the English with the Welsh: "The English fight for power, the Welsh for liberty; the one to procure gain, the other to avoid loss."[20] Clausewitz possessed a thorough understanding of the guerrillas' limitations. So did Giraldus, who insisted that the Welshmen could only be relied upon for one charge and would not sustain a repulse.

Nothing, of course, would be more mistaken than to overemphasize the similarities between the work of a medieval Welsh scholar and a modern Prussian general. Clausewitz's thought on war was much broader in its sweep and more philosophical in its tenor than that of Giraldus Clausewitz, unlike most earlier military writers in Europe, generalized on warfare as a whole. He interpreted war as the continuation of state policy by other means (a doctrine which Lenin later adapted to his purpose by describing war as revolution by other means). But Clausewitz did not think of war as an instrument of popular revolution. Clausewitz, like Giraldus Cambrensis before him, assumed that an invaded

[19] Giraldus Cambrensis, *Itinerary through Wales*, p. 167.

[20] Giraldus Cambrensis, *Itinerary through Wales*, p. 205.

23

people would rally in a national union to expel an invader. Basing his studies on the Napoleonic wars in Europe, Clausewitz held that a subjugated people as a whole might rise to expel an alien conqueror. He concluded therefore that governments battling against an intruder from abroad could safely call on the forces of the national will; partisan warfare could be regarded as a valuable adjunct to the operations of regular armies obedient to constituted authority. Clausewitz did not take account of the incipient impact of industrialization on war. He assumed—most mistakenly—that the technology of war was not likely to change very much in days to come. He looked into the past as much as into the future. His theories sum up, above all, the accumulated military experiences of the age preceding the Industrial Revolution.

2.   Partisan Warfare,
the Industrial Revolution,
and the Heyday of Imperialism

The late eighteenth century witnessed a rapid acceleration of technological development especially in England, where the steam engine was first applied to industrial use. The use of more advanced machinery also spread to parts of France, Belgium, Rhenish Prussia, and other parts of Western Europe. Older cities expanded their population. New manufacturing towns grew apace, as factories provided landless men with new means of employment. Urban unrest acquired increasing political importance as a larger portion of Western Europeans migrated to the towns, as the new industrial working class acquired a greater measure of literacy and of discipline than had been customary among the urban poor in the pre-industrial era.

Revolutionary theorists in Western Europe thus began to look on popular warfare in a different way. They no longer thought in terms of national wars alone. They began to emphasize the divergent interests of different social classes. They increasingly placed their trust in the towns, where they looked to the urban middle and working classes, and thought in terms of urban insurrections. Their model was the French Revolution; their heroes the Jacobins, a predominantly middle-class group that drew much of its strength from Paris.

Most revolutionary thinkers now took inadequate account of the peasants, despite the fact that rural unrest had played an important part in shattering the Bourbon monarchy. Urban intellectuals, a class of increasing political and numerical importance, tended to be insufficiently acquainted with the practical problems of the countryside. They commonly considered the peasants at best as auxiliaries in the coming struggle for power. The peasants were geographically dispersed and often remained wedded to what Marx considered religious superstition. They were harder to assemble and discipline than workmen used to the impersonal routine of a large factory. The peasants' revolutionary aims were generally limited in kind. Servile farmers wished only to be rid of seignorial dues and services and to become small landowners. Once this aim had been achieved, the peasants became a conservative rather than a revolutionary force. When the Parisian workers rose against the newly established Republic in June 1848, French countrymen looked down on the rebellious proletarians as bloodstained anarchists. In the Austro-Hungarian empire, concessions were made to the peasants. Hence the villagers for the most part remained aloof from the revolutionary struggles of 1848. Marx thus bitterly concluded that the smaller Slavonic nationalities of the Austrian Empire were religious-minded reactionaires, backward rural people who had betrayed the revolution. The Slavs of Germany — Marx argued — had long since lost their political vitality; they must perforce follow in the footsteps of their more powerful neighbors. The Welsh in Britain, the Basques in Spain, the French Canadians in North America, the Carinthians, and the Dalmatians were on the way out.[21] The future lay with large nations bent on industrialization.

Marx took a similar attitude toward the colonial peoples. He felt quite convinced that the British in India, for instance, were carrying out a "progressive" function in smashing the precapitalist institutions of the subcontinent; he similarly sympathized with the white settlers in New Zealand, and never worried about the indigenous Maori. The revolutionary future, Marx believed, lay with the industrial workers in the Western cities.

Marx's revolutionary theories, however, were worked out at a time when the conditions for insurrection began to undergo a rapid change. From the purely military point of view the barricade was never a very effective device. Reliance on it entailed tactics of passive defense. Insurgencies up to 1848 were effective when working-class rebels received active or passive support from middle-class national guards, and when the leadership of the government forces had lost its grip and its confidence. From 1849, however, the political

[21] Karl Marx, *Revolution und Kontre-Revolution in Deutschland* (Stuttgart, T. H. W. Dietz, Nachf., 1920), pp. 97-100. Karl Kautsky's preface tries to explain away these sentiments in the light of conditions of 1896.

conditions became more unfavorable. The bourgeoisie usually rallied in support of existing institutions; soldiers no longer saw their opponents as the people, but rather as a gang of looters. In addition, there were important changes in the structure of the city. Revolutionary tacticians in preindustrial cities used to place their trust on barricades that could quickly be thrown up in narrow lanes, and whose construction required no technical skill. These tactics made good sense in preindustrial cities with their winding lanes and dark back-alleys, where the populace could fire muskets from rooftops, hurl stones from windows, and where meandering streets could not easily be swept by artillery. In the older cities of Europe, moreover, the mean hovels of the poor often adjoined the magnificent palaces of the nobility. The various strata of society mingled on the streets, and urban mobs were an ever-present threat. Urban expansion and the development of industries, however, tended to emphasize residential segregation between the various social classes. The factory owners moved away from the vicinity of the factory; the workers became concentrated in huge urban aggregations. Merchants and proletarians no longer lived cheek by jowl. Mob action, whether spontaneous or organized, ceased to be as effective a threat as in the olden days.

Technological development likewise favored established governments. Troops could move much more rapidly by railway than on ill-kept roads. Breech-loading, and later magazine-loading, rifles greatly added to the rapidity and accuracy of an army's firepower. The gunmaker's craft made rapid advances, and engineers perfected their methods of destruction.[22] Changes in city planning greatly favored government forces equipped with the new armaments. Baron Haussman's work in driving straight boulevards through the ancient quarters of Paris is well known. But similar changes were made in scores and scores of minor cities. A street-map of Mainz, a medium-sized city on the middle Rhine, will serve as a perfect case study. The old center was a maze of narrow, little streets. In 1822 the city architect effected a break-

[22] Friedrich Engels, "Neue Bedingungen des bewaffneten Aufstandes," in F. Engels-V. I. Lenin, *Militärpolitische Schriften,* K. Schmidt, ed. (Berlin, Internationaler Arbeiterverlag, 1930), pp. 131-35.

through from the cathedral in the center to the so-called Schillerplatz,[23] thereby completely changing the city's internal strategic situation. The new quarters built east of the *Grosse Bleiche* were planned on a rectangular pattern and follow Haussman's idea. They dominated the main railway station and the new industries; successful insurrectionary fighting in a fine boulevard like the Kaiserstrasse would be extremely difficult.

The nineteenth century also witnessed major changes in police techniques. Perhaps the most far-reaching reforms took place in Great Britain, which may therefore serve as a convenient model. In the eighteenth century the United Kingdom relied for its security on a system of parish constables. This arrangement worked well enough in small villages but broke down completely in great urban centers like London. Two hundred years ago the British capital was virtually unpoliced; vice and violence flourished to an extent that make modern "crime waves" seem like Sunday School outings. British mobs were fearsome aggregations that could be controlled, in the last instance, only by calling out troops and firing into the crowds after great devastation had already taken place. Rich merchants or great noblemen did not fare too badly under this system, since the wealthy hired armed footmen for their defense. Eighteenth-century politicians were not above using mobs for political purposes; the richer rate-payers disliked the idea of spending more money on policemen.

The demand for improved protection came from the ranks of the petty bourgeoisie and from "respectable" working men, who could not afford to pay for their own protection. The campaign for a better police force was supported by men like Francis Place, a Radical, and a tailor by profession, who battled for the rights of labor unions, for Parliamentary reform, and who also invented the technique of massed police baton charges. Police reorganization began in 1829. British reformers introduced ideas adapted from light infantry training in the Peninsula War, and thereby brought about remarkable changes. Within about two decades the British had built up one of the most efficient and humane

---

[23]W. F. Volbach, *Mainz* (Berlin, Deutscher Kunstverlag, 1928), pp. 28-29.

police systems the world had ever known. Their system relied on decentralization and civilian control, and it laid special stress on the preventive role of the police. The new forces were highly visible and yet civilian in status and ethos. They instituted continuous patrols in place of the old system of penal repression.[24] They recruited an excellent body of men from the élite of the lower middle and upper levels of the British working class, who in turn policed the other orders of society, including the *Lumpenproletariat*. The various British police forces generally contained people with a reasonably good education and good moral character, who earned the respect of their fellow countrymen. The police learned the art of coping with mobs by non-lethal means. Rising police standards thus played their part, together with rising living standards and administrative and political reforms, in slaying the specter of a British revolution.

In France, urban insurrections likewise yielded diminishing military returns. The armed city folk of Paris played a vital part in the French Revolution. The revolution of 1830 which, for the second time, defeated a Bourbon regime, likewise had its origins in Paris, though the provinces subsequently assumed control. Gradually, however, Paris began to lose some of its former importance. The extension of the telegraph made the provinces more aware of what was going on in the capital. The construction of railways facilitated the rapid movement of troops and supplies to the capital. When, in June 1848, the urban proletariat of Paris rose against a newly established Republican regime, the provinces unexpectedly came into their own. The French peasants were incensed against what they regarded as a threat against property. The Paris workers constituted but a small minority within the nation at large, and the workers' revolt was overthrown after savage slaughter.

Despite the lessons of the June battle, and despite the warnings issued by Engels and others, many revolutionaries continued to put their trust in urban insurrections. But city-based risings deriving from a few social strata, without support from the country as a whole, were always doomed to

[24] See Patrick Pringle, *Hue and Cry: The Birth of the British Police Force* (London, Museum Press, 1955); and Sir Charles Reith, *A New Study of Police History* (Edinburgh, Oliver and Boyd, 1956).

military failure – whatever intended or unintended political advantages might accrue to the rebels. City-born risings nevertheless retained some political importance, especially when the rebels were able to add luster to their cause by fighting a grim street-battle. After the French were defeated by the forces of a united Germany, Paris in 1871 was shaken by the rising of the Paris Commune. This was a patriotic insurrection directed against an Establishment accused of having betrayed the country to the hated Prussians. The rebels were determined to wage an all-out war, but they had no backing in the provinces, and could not make any headway among the remnants of the defeated French army. The government forces reoccupied Paris, slaughtered their opponents, and inflicted terrible losses on the Parisian proletariat. The Communards did, however, make a profound ideological impact on their age. The French proletarians once again proved that they could wield arms when in desperate circumstances. Equally important was the fact that Marxists who had disapproved of the outbreak when it started won vicarious glory by their subsequent support of the movement. They suddenly acquired a reputation for being red-blooded revolutionaries—a label that has stuck ever since. (Ironically enough, Maoists today still gain inspiration from the Paris Commune, even though the Communards were in no sense Communists, and their program of social reconstruction was sketchy.)

The military, technological, and social revolution that rendered old-fashioned urban insurrections obsolete also helped established governments to enforce order in the most remote rural regions of the European hinterland. "Social bandits" of the Robin Hood and the *Schinderhannes* variety could only prey on the rich in backward areas where communications were poor, and where robbers could rely on support from the poverty-stricken and ignorant peasantry. The railroad engineer, the road builder, and the village schoolmaster in the long run turned out to be even more dangerous to the highwayman than the most enterprising *gendarmes*. By the end of the nineteenth century, "social bandits" of the old-fashioned kind were found only in a few backwaters of Europe such as Sicily and Macedonia. In the end the robber was driven into the city. Western gangsterism today is an urban problem. Today's gangsters depend on city-skills like driving an automobile, opening a safe, manipulating the currency, or practicing graft connected with welfare projects.

The Europeans not only managed to subdue their own backward rural areas; they were equally successful in crushing country-bred warriors in many parts of Africa and Asia. The nineteenth century is indeed the century of the classical "small wars" in the colonies. European troops and their colonial auxiliaries waged "subalterns' wars" against indigenous fighting men on the rough *kopjes* of Matabeleland, on the South African veld, in roadless hill-country on the North-Western Frontier of India, in Burmese jungles, and on drought-ridden Mexican plains.

British theoreticians of war, including a distinguished military historian like Cyril Falls, tend to group all kinds of operations against primitive peoples under the general heading of "small wars." In actual fact, these categories should be sharply distinguished. Many colonial campaigns entailed regular wars against regular armies. For instance, the Matabele, a warlike cattle-keeping warrior people who had established a powerful kingdom in what is now Rhodesia, had regular armies whose training and mobilization depended on a peculiar "age set" system. The Matabele perfected infantry tactics that depended on tight discipline, rapid movement, and the shock effect of masses of spearmen charging in close formation. The Matabele won many victories over their neighbors, but their tactics became ossified. The Matabele made insufficient use of firearms. Their generals were in some ways oddly like their opposite numbers in British Guards Regiments. They placed too much emphasis on the cult of cold steel, on the pomp and circumstance of military might, on the elaborate splendor of the "Great Dance" (in some ways like a great troop review), on the magnificence of gorgeous plumed headdresses, and on other unessential appurtenances of war.

In 1893 the Matabele armies were overthrown by British settlers, who pitted mounted riflemen and automatic weapons against great masses of infantry armed primarily with assegais, knobkerries, and ox-hide shields. It was only when the Matabele had suffered defeat that they turned to partisan warfare against the whites and began to make more effective use of firearms. So did the supposedly unwarlike Mashona, the erstwhile foes and victims of the Matabele, who proved even more adept at guerrilla operations than their Matabele neighbors.

Between 1896 and 1897, the British nevertheless effectively subjugated Rhodesia. In other parts of the world, white troops and their indigenous auxiliaries were equally successful against tribal warriors. Throughout the nineteenth century, Europeans and Americans had indeed to contend with partisan warfare of the most variegated kind. American cavalrymen, for instance, battled against such opponents as the Apache, perhaps the most skillful guerrillas of world history. They were a people completely specialized in the art of warfare. Their warriors were brilliant horsemen and deadly shots, who could live off the land, make a quick get-away on captured horses, and who knew how to use to perfection every ruse of warfare and every artifice of camouflage. British soldiers battled against Somali desert warriors mounted on camels, against Ashanti soldiers seeking cover in the tropical forests of the Gold Coast, and against Pathani partisans operating in roadless hills.

By and large, white or white-led troops won in such encounters. It was only on such rare occasions as when they had to seek out the foe in remote mountain country where the terrain placed impossible obstacles in the invaders' way that they suffered defeat. Much of the Europeans' initial advantage depended on superior organization, on better-organized supply services, on tighter discipline, and on superior leadership. Of course the white soldiers had better weapons too. They had factory-made guns and rifles. But the technological factor should not be overestimated. In many colonial campaigns, distance and difficult terrain precluded the effective use of artillery. The development of rifles was relatively slow. The first efficient breechloader was the Prussian needle gun, adopted in 1848. In 1867 a British officer devised a rolled metal cartridge, and in 1871 the British adopted the single-loading Henry-Martini rifle. Smokeless powder and repeating rifles only came into use in the latter part of the nineteenth century, a major step forward being the construction of the Mauser rifle with bolt action and a charger-loaded magazine. Many colonial insurgents moreover managed to acquire modern European rifles. Others bought weapons discarded by European armies. The more modern and expensive arms went to wealthier people like some of the Arab slave traders on the East African coast. The most out-of-date weapons went to the most backward tribes, people like the Bemba of northeastern Rhodesia, who, by the end of the nineteenth century, were found to be well-armed with the British "Tower Musket," which had once done duty for Wellington's veterans.

The most decisive technical innovations affecting "small wars," however, only came toward the end of the nineteenth century. Especially important was the fully automatic gun, a weapon similar to the Maxim which African tribesmen could neither buy nor service. The automatic gun did not, however, come into use until the early 1890s, when British settlers first employed Maxims against the Matabele of Southern Rhodesia. This meant that throughout most of the nineteenth century Europeans usually had only a limited superiority in firepower. The same holds true in the field of transport. In many cases European troops gained considerable assistance from steam power applied to railways and ships. Steam power might greatly affect the strategy of a colonial war, but it rarely influenced its tactics.[25] Throughout the nineteenth century, colonial forces lacking motorized transport generally depended on their ability to outmarch their opponents in battle. Nevertheless, the colonial powers generally managed to cope with indigenous resistance movements; anti-colonial guerrillas were successfully crushed.

One of the most important guerrilla wars of the nineteenth century was that waged against the French in Algeria. In 1830 a French army disembarked in Algeria, where the French supplanted the country's previous Turkish overlords. But effective pacification took more than half a century. The Muslim people had a long tradition of battle against the infidel; many of them were well armed and were determined to resist both foreign control and white settlement. The Algerians found a magnificent leader in Abd-el-Kader, the Emir of Mascara, a man well learned in theology and

[25] There were a few exceptions. In the Boer war the British used armored trains against Boer commandos operating in Bechuanaland.

philosophy. He was full of religious enthusiasm, yet favorable to Westernizing reforms of the kind carried out by Mehemet Ali in Egypt. Abd-el-Kader drew both on religious and on national loyalties. He also gained the support of peasants fearful for their land rights. He had his own artillery park, and he gathered a regular force of paid janissaries that even contained deserters from the French Foreign Legion. There was bitter fighting, and the fortunes of war only began to shift in the French favor when Thomas-Robert Bugeaud, a one-time grenadier in Napoleon's army, obtained command. Bugeaud, a brilliant soldier, abandoned the system of scattering small forces in blockhouses, where the men became victims to sickness, boredom, and enemy raids. He organized instead flying columns, and introduced small mountain guns that were carried into the interior by mules. Wheeled transport was practically eliminated, and the army thenceforth relied on horses, mules, and camels instead of on slow-moving wagons. Bugeaud became a master of counter-guerrilla tactics. He also used the *razzia*, the swift, ruthless punishment raid on offending villages where crops were burnt and cattle seized, thus depriving enemy guerrillas of supplies. Bugeaud effectively kept the enemy on the move. His operations benefited greatly from his study of Roman practice. The French, with unshaken cultural self-confidence, regarded their work as a revival of Rome's ancient civilizing mission, and gained the initiative not merely in military but also in economic and administrative affairs. The *Bureau Arabe*, an efficient administrative and political body, effectively administered the conquered territory. Bugeaud built a network of roads and encouraged European settlement. Bugeaud also had, what his predecessors lacked, an army of 100,000 men, a tremendous force by the standards of nineteenth-century Africa. Abd-el-Kader's forces, on the other hand, were riddled by tribal dissensions. The Berber Muslims suffered heavy losses as the French destroyed the crops and seized the cattle of disaffected Algerians. In 1847, after bitter and sustained resistance, Abd-el-Kader was forced to surrender.[26]

[26] There is an extensive literature on the subject. See, for instance, Camille Rousset, *La Conquête de l'Algérie,* 2 vols. (Paris, Librairie Plon, 1904); and Marcel Emerit, *L'Algérie a l'époque d' Abd-el-Kader (Paris, Editions Larose, 1951).*

Algeria became a nursery of French guerrilla warfare experts, men like Marshal Bazaine, who did brilliant work in counterinsurgency operations, though they subsequently often proved a complete failure in regular warfare against the Germans.[27] In 1862, at a time when the United States was engaged in civil war, the French intervened in Mexico in defense of French financial interests. In 1863 French troops under Bazaine occupied Mexico City; and Maximilian, a Habsburg archduke, became Emperor of Mexico by the grace of France and the Mexican clerical party. The scattered troops loyal to the country's republican institutions fought on in guerrilla fashion, ill-supported, largely unpaid, and lacking a unified command. The Mexican guerrillas found an able leader in Benito Juárez, who organized resistance in the north and controlled a large portion of the country. Bazaine, however, solved his problems in an admirable fashion. He had learned the art of war in the hard North African school, and he refused to dissipate his strength in pursuing stray *guerrilleros* or in holding the wide front from the Gulf of Mexico to the Pacific. Instead he concentrated his army against the main Mexican forces in the north, leaving the smaller bands to be mopped up later. The French and Maximilian's Mexican forces were organized in two flying columns of the same type as Bugeaud's standard columns in Algeria. The French expertly pushed the republicans into the desolate country lying between Mexico and the United States, in much the same way as Abd-el-Kader had been pushed out of the more populous portions of Algeria.

From the military point of view, the French were making headway. In the political sphere, however, they were less successful. Maximilian failed to obtain genuinely popular support in Mexico. Worse still, he failed to secure recognition from the United States. As long as Americans were locked in a bitter civil war, this did not matter. But once Lee surrendered, the French position became untenable. Napoleon III could not face conflict with a great war-hardened American army, and the Mexican venture became

[27] See Philip Guedalla, *The Two Marshals:Bazaine, Pétain* (New York, Reynal and Hitchcock, 1943).

bitterly unpopular in France itself. The French withdrew, leaving Maximilian to his fate.[28]

The greatest nineteenth-century partisan war was fought in South Africa. In 1899 hostilities broke out between Great Britain on the one hand and the Transvaal Republic and the Orange Free State on the other. The prize of victory was political supremacy in South Africa, and the war became in many ways a watershed in British military history. The conflict began as a small colonial affair, an imperial venture of the "limited liability" variety, financed on a shoestring, and fought against an enemy hardly considered superior to warlike Indian mountaineers. It ended as the greatest British military effort hitherto made on land. Nearly 450,000 soldiers ultimately served on the British side. Of these some 53,000 men were white South Africans (mostly English-speaking) whose presence on the battlefield gave to the conflict something of the character of a South African civil war, comparable in some respects to other nineteenth-century wars of unification.

The Boer War, which had begun as an armed clash, fought in the traditional manner according to fixed rules, designed to protect civilians and to confine hostilities to military specialists, concluded as a half-way house to total war. Civilians were rounded up, farms were burnt, and effective though unintended steps were taken to wreck the economy on which the Boer War effort depended. The Boers never mobilized more than some 87,000 men. However, they were superior in mobility and marksmanship to the British. They fought as irregular cavalry and they excelled in partisan operations. They were magnificent tacticians, but they lacked strategists. Their command structure remained loose; their forces lacked cohesion. Instead of pursuing a war of movement and invading the Cape Province, the Boers needlessly locked up large bodies of men in sieges which they had neither the will nor the means to bring to a successful conclusion.

[28] For the Mexican side see Juan de Dios Arías, *Reseña histórica de la formación y operciones del cuerpo de Ejército del Norte durante la intervención francesa* (Mexico, N. Chavez, 1867), and Gustave Léon Nion, *Expédition du Mexique, 1861-1867 . . .* (Paris, J. Dumaine, 1874).

The British also suffered from many weaknesses. The despatch of nearly 400,000 men to fight on the other side of the world was admittedly a great organizational achievement, something never previously attempted in history by any power. In every other respect, however, British military planning failed to meet the occasion. Operations initially were marked by lack of co-ordination and also by inefficiency in the decentralization of command. There were never enough maps. Intelligence before, and scouting during, operations were usually inadequate. The Boers had the good fortune to fight at a time just before the combustion engine had revolutionized the art of war. Had the Boer War broken out twenty years later, armored cars and aircraft, supported by motorized infantry and mechanized supply services, would swiftly have put an end to the depredations of horsemen on the open veld. As it was, the British over and over again launched disastrous frontal attacks against a well-entrenched enemy possessing great and accurate firepower. The British Lee-Metford rifle of .303 caliber was no match for the German clip-loading .275-inch Mauser used by the Boers. From the very start the British had some excellent mounted infantry such as the Cape Mounted Rifles and the Rhodesia Regiment. Nevertheless they all too often tried to fight a highly mobile enemy with slow-moving infantry.

In the end the British won by a combination of blockhouse cordons and mounted sweeps. They systematically destroyed Boer farms, used by the enemy as supply centers for mobile columns. They interned the civilian homeless, though they abstained from executing captured *franc tireurs*, as Continental armies were wont to do. The Boer commandoes were kept on the move, worn down and defeated in detail. The British followed up their victories by setting up an effective administrative machine and an efficient police organization, and by financing reconstruction. At long last in 1902 the Boers agreed to make peace.[29]

These colonial operations took place at different times between very different opponents. Nevertheless the campaigns have certain features in common. Boers, Algerians, and

[29] For the most authoritative account of the war, see L. Amery, ed., *The Times History of the War in South Africa 1899-1902*, 7 vols. (London, Sampson, Low, Marston and Co., 1900-1909).

Mexicans were all tough fighting men, inured to hardships and knowledgeable about field craft. The guerrillas were mobile and believed passionately in their cause. Yet they all had similar weaknesses. The partisan forces were composed mainly of countrymen; their strength lay in the rural areas. All suffered from severe internal divisions. The Algerians had to contend with tribal differences. The Boers suffered from an inefficient council-of-war system which itself reflected their entire socio-political structure, with its insistence on decentralization and popular control. The Mexicans were divided by a host of political and provincial disagreements. None of the movements in question possessed permanent revolutionary cadres. The guerrillas generally lacked the technical skills of the city. There were of course many exceptions; Boer artillery, sometimes stiffened by German or other foreign volunteers, usually gave an excellent account of itself, and their imported Krupp guns were responsible for many casualties among the British. But when it came to constructing or storming defense works, Boer farmers could hardly compete with the British miners and technicians who turned Kimberley, for instance, into an impregnable stronghold.

Social issues played a considerable part in all these small wars. But except for the Haitians, none of the guerrillas had a master plan for completely reshaping society. (Even the Haitian slave leaders were by no means united in the hatred of forced labor; Dessalines and other insurrectionary leaders at first forced peasants to continue working on sugar plantations, so as to raise some revenue for the new state.) The Boers were mainly farmers. They wished to carry on their own way of life, while at the same time gaining the utmost advantage from the British-controlled gold industry. It is sheer romanticism, therefore, to regard the Boers as bewildered herdsmen at war with a capitalist system that they did not understand and that they opposed. This was the line mistakenly taken both by British imperialists of the period and by liberal and socialist critics of imperialism at the time. President Kruger, the Transvaal head of state, of course stood for the interests of the Boer farming communities. But he did not want to destroy the mining industry; he did not wish to expropriate the British-owned mines; nor did he wish to drive the uitlanders into the sea. He wanted to tax the foreigners, but to keep political power in the hands of his own people.

In Mexico the war against the French had social implications. Maximilian was backed by churchmen and large landowners. The Liberals were wedded to reforms that would divest the church of lands not solely devoted to religious purposes. Juárez was a peasant's son, and wished to defend the rights of poor Indians against the great *hacendados*. But Juárez did not think in terms of all-out social revolution, and once he attained power his reforms remained modest in character.

The Algerians and their like moreover failed to secure effective allies on a large scale within the so-called imperialist countries. In nineteenth-century France there were many critics of colonial expansion. But those who denigrated French or British policy in Africa were more concerned with the financial expenditure and the diversion of military manpower than with general ethical principles. Few nineteenth-century Europeans believed colonial conquest at the expense of more backward races was inherently immoral. The Europeans in Africa felt that they alone represented the progressive forces of history: that Algerians and Zulus, Matabele or Somali stood for the past; they were remote; they might be romantic, but they were wrong.

European colonizers in the nineteenth century were therefore willing to accept much heavier losses than were their descendants. In Southern Rhodesia, for instance, the British, between 1896 and 1897, had to cope with a major native rising. The settlers lost something like ten percent of their numbers, a staggeringly high figure, infinitely higher than the proportion of casualties suffered by white colonists in the Algerian national rising or the Mau Mau war in Kenya in the mid-twentieth century. The technological discrepancy between "Imperial" forces and their partisan opponents in the nineteenth century was much less than that which existed between a mid-twentieth century "colonialist" army (supplied with tracked vehicles, helicopters, fighter bombers, transport planes, and walkie-talkie sets) and modern partisans. But in the Rhodesia of the 1890s the colonists' will to rule remained unbroken. They felt that history was on their side, that Europe stood behind them, and that they formed the vanguard of civilization in Darkest Africa. The European clergymen and missionaries in the country, the only element approaching a local intelligentsia, were as full of fight as their fellow-settlers. There was none to sympathize with the insurgents or to call for concessions in the cause of peace. Moreover, the settlers' estimate of themselves was generally shared by public opinion at home. The Europeans enjoyed complete moral ascendancy over their opponents, whose resistance was perhaps born of despair more than of any belief in ultimate victory.[30]

From the political point of view the Boer War formed a borderline case. The Boers, unlike Mexicans, Algerians, or Mashona, were a European people. Their cause aroused immense sympathy on the entire European continent. In Britain itself there was a pro-Boer party. British humanitarians condemned what they called British "methods of barbarism." Catholic conservatives like Hilaire Belloc and humanitarian radicals like John Atkinson Hobson denounced hook-nosed "Rand Lords" for whose profits the war was supposedly being fought. Hobson's experience as a newspaper correspondent in South Africa turned him against imperialism in general. His hatred of Milner's methods soon broadened into a major critique of imperialism that in turn greatly influenced Lenin.[31] (In South Africa itself, one of the founders of the local Communist Party was Sidney Percival Bunting, a disillusioned upper-class Englishman, who had originally come to Africa as a volunteer to fight the Boers, and whom the war turned into a pacifist.) In the British Isles, disenchantment with the Boer War played a major part in weaning educated British people away from imperialism; but as long as hostilities lasted, British national feeling was strong enough to insist on unconditional victory, and the Boers were crushed.

Given freedom from outside intervention, the imperial forces always prevailed in the end. The French faced no

---

[30] L. H. Gann, *A History of Southern Rhodesia: Early Days to 1934* (London, Chatto and Windus, 1965), pp. 129-39.

[31] See John Atkinson Hobson, *Imperialism: A Study* (London, George Allen and Unwin, 1902).

foreign enemy in the Abd-el-Kader campaign. They did not, however, dare to challenge the United States in Mexico. Superior sea power allowed the British to defy all foreign sympathizers with the Boers. The imperial forces always had to learn the hard lesson that guerrillas cannot be fought by methods of static defense alone, but only by mobile columns employing aggressive tactics.

Military victories as such, however, were meaningless unless the colonizers exploited their success by means of effective occupation. It was in this area that Bugeaud was a master. In war he stressed the use of surprise to weaken the enemy and the value of political warfare to disrupt the opponent's cohesion. But once victory was in his grasp he also knew how to govern, and thereby effectively pacified vast areas of Algeria by means of methods deliberately copied from the ancient Romans. Bugeaud's methods were further developed by General Joseph Simon Gallieni, who made his name in Indochina and Madagascar at the end of the last century. Gallieni stressed in particular that the army must improve the social condition of the indigenous peoples and improve their standard of life. "Every time that the necessities of war force one of our colonial officers to take action against a village or an inhabited center, his first concern, once submission of the inhabitants has been achieved, should be the reconstruction of the village, creation of a market, and establishment of a school."[32]

Gallieni's pupil Lyautey further applied this technique in Morocco. According to Lyautey, "military occupation consists less in military operations than in an organization on the march." Administration should not be set up behind the front as a kind of afterthought. On the contrary, the administrators should march in step with the advancing soldiers. The new organization should be an effective network covering the whole area. Administrative details should be worked out in advance. Government should be entrusted to men specially trained for the purpose. "The occupation," he argued, "deposits the units on the soil like

[32] Jean Gottmann, "Bugeaud, Galliéni, Lyautey: The Development of French Colonial Warfare," in *Makers of Modern Strategy: Military Thought from Machiavelli to Hitler,* Edward Mead Earle *et al.,* eds. (New York, Atheneum, 1966), pp. 234-59, esp. p. 242 and p. 243.

sedimentary strata." Hence, spectacular clashes of arms should be avoided as far as possible. The army should conciliate rather than terrorize, stress political and military more than economic achievements, build rather than destroy. The strategy of "search, destroy, withdraw" (popularly known in the British Indian Army at the time as the strategy of "butcher and bolt") was ineffectual. Conquest entailed effective administration with a purpose. These theories were fully in accord with Clausewitz's philosophy concerning war as policy by other means. They prescribed and also summed up Franco-British military practice in the colonies in its most advanced state. They were reapplied in certain ways, with totally different means, within a totally different context, and with totally different aims by the anti-colonial forces that later liquidated French rule in Algeria and Indochina.

3. Partisan Warfare in the First Third of the Twentieth Century

Colonial warfare played an important part in the history of the nineteenth and early twentieth centuries. But European revolutionaries — for all their militant oratory — did not generally display much interest in the strategy of resistance movements or of insurrectionary struggles in the backward parts of the world. Throughout the nineteenth century there were few socialist theoreticians of guerrilla warfare. The foremost white practitioners of "small wars" were to be found, not among the ranks of left wingers in Western Europe, but among Balkan *comitadji* (guerrillas) of the nationalist variety. The Christian *comitadji* originally struggled against their Turkish overlords and gradually helped to break the Ottoman Empire in Europe. But once victory against the infidel seemed in sight, partisans often began to turn their arms against rival Christian nationalities. Poverty-stricken, ethnically mixed areas like Macedonia became the scene of ferocious excesses. As long as Macedonia remained under Ottoman suzerainty, Serbs, Bulgarians, and Greeks all came to be convinced that they would have to preempt the future by armed action. Supported by their respective mother countries, Greek, Serbian, and especially Bulgarian gangs began a campaign of intimidation and terror against villagers with a different ethnic affiliation. Guerrilla warfare turned into a means of national self-assertion and of "converting" the members of other ethnic groups. For this purpose, the village schoolmaster, the priest, and the guerrilla chief commonly worked hand in hand. The modern notion of using guerrillas as a Fifth Column, of infiltrating partisans into disputed borderlands, of creating guerrilla zones where there is neither peace nor war, owes a great deal to the precedent set up by Balkan fighters before World War I.

Other European experts in the art of waging small wars were found among a very different group, among imaginative British, French, and German army officers. In the previous section we have referred to the contribution made by Gallieni and Lyautey to the art of conducting colonial wars. European officers, however, also adopted guerrilla methods at times as a means of fighting conventional opponents in the colonial world. One of the most successful of these was General Paul Emil von Lettow-Vorbeck, commander of the German forces in East Africa during World War I. Lettow-Vorbeck's political ideals were archaic. But as a military technician he was brilliant. His operations against the Allies still rank as the model of an irregular campaign, conducted by professional troops in difficult bush country against overwhelming odds.

Equally outstanding was T. E. Lawrence, or "Lawrence of Arabia," who helped to organize an Arab national rising against the Turks during World War I. His object was to support the British army in the Near East. The British in turn gave some assistance to the Arabs, and Arab fighting men set out on a guerrilla campaign that combined the military traditions of nomadic desert warriors with modern industrial skills. Lawrence relied on Arab raiding forces, on warlike tribesmen mounted on camels but equipped with light automatics and high explosives. The mounted Arab guerrilla, like his Boer equivalent in the South African War at the turn of the century, was fortunate in operating at a period just before the application of the internal combustion engine to war had rendered traditional cavalry almost obsolete. Had the Turks been equipped with aircraft and armored cars, like the British in Iraq during the postwar era, they could have dominated the desert and crushed their nomad enemies. But the Turks were still dependent on railways, on the technology of the pre-gasoline age. Their supply system in the Arabian Peninsula was vulnerable, and Arab partisans used their opportunities with superb skill. They struck at the rear of the Turkish forces; they disrupted railway communications; they hit at the enemy's weak rather than at his strong points; they pinned down large forces in a few garrisons, and they finally wore out the Turks' will to resist.

Lawrence based his strategy on the assumption that the Turks would not be able to control effectively the vast territories under their sway. Guerrillas, forever elusive, without front or rear, drifting around like a cloud of gas,

44

would always be able to get the better of a regular occupation force tied down to cumbersome supply lines. Lawrence believed in economy of manpower. He concentrated on the destruction of matériel rather than of men, and shaped Arab tribesmen into highly mobile striking forces. These moved in the desert like ships in the sea, and were virtually invulnerable to the enemy's counterblows. Lawrence was keenly aware of the importance of supplies. Indeed he argued that the invention of bully beef had revolutionized land warfare more than the invention of gunpowder. Provided the guerrillas played their cards correctly, he argued, and provided conditions were suitable, the partisans could win without support from a big army. The success of a rebellion depended on an unassailable base, such as the Arabs had in the Red Sea ports and the desert. The partisans could beat a highly sophisticated, well-disciplined enemy army, provided they could adjust mobility to space. The enemy forces had to be too few to dominate the whole combat area effectively from fortified posts. Guerrillas needed a friendly population. Rebellions could be made if only two percent of the people served in the striking force, and ninety-eight percent were passively sympathetic. The partisans required speed, endurance, ubiquity, and independence of supply arteries. They required sufficient technical equipment to destroy the enemy's communications and the ability to strike swiftly where the enemy was not. "Granted mobility, security (in the form of denying targets to the enemy), time and doctrine (the idea to convert every subject to friendliness) victory will rest with the insurgents, for the algebraical factors are in the end decisive, and against them perfections of means and spirit struggle quite in vain."[33]

In planning for world revolution, Marxist theoreticians might have been expected to take some account of Lawrence's military theory and of colonial guerrilla warfare in general. The great majority of French, British, and German communists, however, were essentially Eurocentric, more so even than their imperialist opponents. The more radical-

---

[33] Quoted from an entry entitled "Guerrilla" by T. E. Lawrence, in *Encyclopaedia Britannica,* 14th ed., 1929, X, 953. See also T. E. Lawrence, *Seven Pillars of Wisdom, a Triumph* (London, J. Cape, 1935), *passim.*

minded European Marxists agreed that Western colonial empires must be smashed. But they generally believed that the job would be done mainly in Europe, by the Western proletariat. Imperialism, in their view, would have to be destroyed at its center, not at its periphery. Few theoreticians of the class war thus displayed much interest in the technique of guerrilla warfare in the backward parts of the world.

Under the impact of Lenin, however, revolutionary socialists introduced into their strategy a number of far-reaching changes of a more general kind. These were based above all on the Russian experience. Lenin particularly stressed the need for tightly knit party cadres. These alone, in his view, could provide insurgents with the organization required alike in war and in peace. According to Lenin, the bourgeoisie had outlived its formerly progressive role; bourgeois capitalism had turned to imperialism to resolve its internal contradictions; imperialism was bound to lead to more wars. The capitalists had ceased to be the vanguard of society and had instead become parasites on the body politic. Capitalism could not be reformed, but only overthrown by violent means. The revolution must be organized by a highly disciplined party, a combination between a secular church, a crusading order, and a conspiratorial movement. The workers, Lenin argued, did not spontaneously become revolutionary socialists. Left to themselves the proletariat of all countries would only develop a labor-union consciousness, strike for higher wages, and compel the government to pass reform legislation. But this was not enough. The workers needed a permanent general staff and a revolutionary "officer corps," to whom the struggle was alike a vocation, a livelihood, and a way of life. The new party élite would supply the masses both with the leadership and with the ideology that the hour demanded. The party cadres' superior training would enable them both to chart the future and to shape the world to come in their own image.

Whether in fighting or in politics, Lenin believed in a strategy of extreme flexibility. In the military field, he wrote in 1906, Marxism would have to learn from the masses rather than teach the proletariat tactics elaborated by armchair strategists. Combat would assume numerous forms. There would be selective terror through the assassination of high officials and lower-ranking members of the army and police. In addition, revolutionaries would "confiscate" money both from government and from private persons. The *déclassé* elements of the population, the *Lumpenproletariat* and anarchist groups, chose this kind of warfare as the main, or indeed as the only, form of the social war. Marxists could not afford to be squeamish and must adopt similar tactics in case of need. But the Marxists must aim at bringing such actions under the strict control of the party; "confiscations" must not be allowed to degenerate into private gangsterism. The tactics of civil war could not, however, be confined to individual actions. A revolutionary party had to be willing to use every possible expedient — demonstrations, strikes, and street fighting. City-centered "partisan" operations could never be the only, or even the chief, means of the struggle. In so far as Lenin was thinking in terms of an armed struggle, he envisaged primarily operations on the part of city workers, supported or led by city-bred intellectuals.

Lenin nevertheless was willing to allot an important subsidiary role to other forms of armed action. In a period of political general strikes, the uprising could not assume the traditional form of a single blow aiming at the seizure of power in the capital. War might have to be conceived as a protracted form of civil commotion enmeshing the whole country, with a series of big battles, punctuated by a large number of small-scale engagements on the periphery. The Social Democratic (later the Communist) Party's job was to become the party of militancy, which would take the leading part in civil wars.[34]

Lenin turned out to be one of the greatest revolutionary protagonists of the twentieth century. But the actual course of revolution did not conform to the pattern he had anticipated. The tsarist armies and the tsarist state prestige were broken not so much by internal risings but by a series of disastrous defeats in World War I. The victorious Germans then imposed the crushing peace of Brest-Litovsk which, if

---

[34]V. I. Lenin, "Der Partisanenkrieg," in *Proletarij,* 13 October (30 September) 1906, no. 5 (X, 80), reprinted in German in F. Engels-V. I. Lenin, *Militärpolitische Schriften* (Berlin, Internationaler Arbeiter Verlag, 1930), pp. 94-105.

carried out, would probably have prevented the recovery of Russia's great-power status. The Germans, however, were vanquished in turn by the Western Allies. Germany's collapse on the battlefield nullified the effects of the Russian military collapse, giving what might be called an unearned increment of power to the victorious communists. Lenin's followers in the meantime had seized control in a disorganized country and had become involved in a lengthy civil war against "White" armies.

The campaigns against the counterrevolution were waged in the main by organized means. Both "Whites" and "Reds" organized forces of considerable size. The Bolsheviks won through superior discipline and organization, and also because they were able to operate strategically on internal lines. Partisan operations in the countryside played a more limited part in the campaigns. The Bolsheviks in the main put their trust in the urban proletariat, and looked upon the peasantry and discontented ethnic minorities as adjuncts to the city-bred forces of revolution. Lenin hoped that the Russian Revolution would set off similar risings in Western Europe — above all in Germany — but Bolshevism could not prevail in the field against popular Polish nationalism. German communist attempts to seize power by armed coups in big cities all came to nought, and the Russian Revolution remained isolated.

Lenin at the same time took a tough line against ethnic minorities who desired to secede from the Russian state and who at times employed guerrilla tactics for this purpose. Lenin, in theory, believed in mobilizing the backward peoples of Russia against the Tsar and the colonial peoples against Western capitalists. But Lenin's policy in some respects did not mark as much of a break with the past as his admirers were apt to imagine. In trying to stir up discontented peoples against his enemies, Lenin merely followed in the footsteps of legitimate rulers, who had not hesitated to use subversive groups against dynastic opponents abroad. In Russia itself, a country where ethnic minorities accounted for something like half of the total population, Lenin, for all practical purposes, was as much of a centralizer as the tsars. The minorities might enjoy formal constitutional and cultural privileges and even the paper right of secession. But what was justified during the period of imperialism became intolerable under the rule of communism. Lenin believed in a centralized state and a centralized party; he would have nothing to do with a plethora of independent communist parties each seeking its own road to socialism. In 1913 Lenin had already identified his position with that of the Jacobins, the French revolutionary centralizers, against that of the Girondins, the advocates of the provinces against Paris.[35] Lenin did not want to see the breakup of Russia into smaller states. He and his comrades in arms took the most rigorous steps to crush what he called bourgeois nationalist deviations. Except in Russia's western borderlands, these endeavors proved largely successful.

For all their propagandistic efforts, the Soviets made little headway in the Western colonies during the inter-war period. In Africa, for instance, the first communist parties, those of Egypt, Algeria, and South Africa, owed their creation largely to local Europeans. They failed to convert the masses, and none of the African insurgents during the inter-war period fought under the banner of orthodox Marxism-Leninism.

The 1920s nevertheless witnessed a number of risings on what might be called the rural periphery of Europe. Because these incidents had profound long-run effects on twentieth-century history, they merit more attention than would be warranted by the actual scale of military operations. In Morocco, for instance, a rural rebellion broke out against the Spanish government that held sway in the country's northern strip. Mohammed ben Abd-el-Krim, the leader of the rising, was the son of a local kaid, who had worked his way up in the Spanish administration; Abd-el-Krim's brother was educated as a mining engineer. In 1921 the people of the Rif inflicted a crushing defeat on the Spaniards and nearly captured the city of Melilla. In 1924 the Spaniards were compelled to abandon all their inland positions and retreat on Tetuan. By the end of the year, however, Abd-el-Krim became engaged in hostilities against the French, too, and by the middle of the following year he was threatening Fez itself.

---

[35] M. K. Dziewanowski, *Joseph Pilsudski: A European Federalist, 1918-1922* (Stanford, Calif., Hoover Institution Press, 1969), p. 68.

Abd-el-Krim's rising was more than just a tribal affray. His men combined, to some extent, modern skills with more traditional ones. The insurgents learned how to use machine guns and artillery; they manufactured hand grenades from air force bombs. Among the Rif were to be found numerous Jewish artisans, goldsmiths, and metal workers, who found little difficulty in turning their skills to the manufacture of bombs and the repair of guns. Many of the Rif fighting force besides were men with combat experience in the French army. The insurgents learned how to build field telephones, how to construct machine-gun posts, how to camouflage their positions. Because military technology was much less developed in the 1920s than it is today, the French superiority in armored cars was of no avail; and bombing from the air, employed only on a small scale by modern standards, had little effect in a country devoid of towns or factories. The Moroccan villager, moreover, could easily reconstruct his simple villages; and he was an expert at concealing guns in mountain caves.[36] Abd-el-Krim maintained a permanent force of some 7,000 to 8,000 men, who were used as a general reserve and as a stiffening for tribal levies. The main part of the fighting was done by local sympathizers who harried the French from every side. In the end the French were able to mobilize a massive force of 160,000 men under Marshal Pétain. New Spanish troops also disembarked on the coast; and in 1926 Abd-el-Krim, outnumbered and completely isolated, threw in the sponge. The Moroccan rising had failed.

Yet the insurrection is likely to occupy an importance place in the history of guerrilla warfare. It stood half-way between anti-colonial resistance movements of the traditional kind and anti-colonial wars of the modern variety. Abd-el-Krim considered himself to be descended from one of the successors of the Prophet; he played on tribal rivalries; he took the title of Emir. But he also attempted to set up a semimodern state, which he styled the Republic of the Rif. He played his cards with great skill, and the cost of

---

[36] Colonel Bode, *Abd el Krim's Freiheitskampf gegen Franzosen und Spanier* (Berlin, Verlag Offene Worte, 1926), pp. 19-24. The most recent work is David S. Woolman, *Rebels in the Rif: Abd el Krim and the Rif Rebellion* (Stanford University Press, 1968).

suppressing his rising was extremely high. To subsequent revolutionary leaders like Mao Tse-tung, the Moroccan insurrection stood out as an important example of "national guerrilla" warfare.[37] Abd-el-Krim's rising differed from earlier colonial campaigns in North Africa in that the insurgents gained substantial support in France as well as in Morocco. French communists and socialists denounced the French campaign as imperialist banditry serving none but the interests of French capitalists. German nationalists, for very different reasons, also backed Abd-el-Krim. Even the British seem to have favored the Moroccan cause to some extent. Abd-el-Krim was not, however, strong enough to secure victory. The Rif were after all a far-away people of whom the bulk of Europeans knew nothing.

The Irish rising against the British, initiated soon after World War I, followed a very different pattern. For the first time in history a great power, victorious in a world war, possessed of tremendous industrial and military resources, had become so war-weary that it could no longer offer effective resistance to small partisan formations operating in an isolated island wholly enfolded by Britain's unchallenged naval might. The Irish rising marked a milestone in military history; it gained warm approval from Lenin, and it became an inspiration to revolutionaries of a later generation in Palestine, in Cyprus, and in Algeria.

The antecedents of the Irish independence movement are too complicated to be easily summarized. Suffice it to say that the movement contained elements of both a national war of liberation and a civil war. The Irish people were split into what might be called two protonationalities whose origins were defined by differing religious, historical, and cultural traditions. Indeed the first to organize illegal formations were the Protestant Ulstermen, who were determined to resist absorption into an independent and united Ireland, and to whom we shall make reference in a subsequent section.

In southern Ireland the insurgents drew their main strength from Catholics, though their adherents also included some Protestants. The Irish rebels also gained some supporters of

[37]Mao Tse-tung, *On Guerrilla Warfare*, trans. Samuel B. Griffith (New York, Frederick A. Praeger, 1961), p. 49.

wholly or partly English descent. On the other hand, a good many Irish Catholics fought under the Union Jack, so that the struggle to some extent cut across national and religious divisions. The insurgents appealed to Catholic workers in the towns (though not to Protestant proletarians in Belfast, Ireland's main industrial city at the time). Intellectuals, intoxicated with the idea of a splendid Celtic revival, joined the rebel ranks. So did many unemployed people, men who in normal circumstances might have emigrated to the United States or to Australia, but whom the Great War had left stranded in their own country. In addition, agrarian unrest was endemic in many rural areas where tenants were locked in dispute with their landlords. The rebels remembered ancient as well as present grievances; they fought for twenty acres a man and for a glorious future. The better-off farmers had at first usually stood aloof. The British had enjoyed considerable success in their professed policy of "killing Home Rule by kindness" and by rural reforms. But the "Ascendancy" made one mistake after another. In 1916 they crushed the abortive "Easter Rising" in Dublin, but turned the captured rebels into martyrs by executing their leaders. In 1918 the British, hard pressed on the Western Front, proposed to apply conscription in Ireland, and thereby convinced the non-political Irish, especially the farmers and also the Catholic hierarchy, that independence was indeed worth having.

Irish revolutionary tactics merged the skills not only of the soldier and the deer-stalker, the gunman and the mechanic, but also those of the judge, the politician, the publicity expert, and even the travel agent. In the military sphere the Irish built up a partisan organization known as the Irish Republican Army (IRA). According to Michael Collins, an outstanding Irish leader, the IRA's effective strength never exceeded 3,000 men at any one time. It operated in very small formations. The tactical unit was the company of 26 to 100 men; four to seven companies were grouped into battalions; three to six battalions made up a brigade. Supreme authority rested with the General Headquarters Staff at Dublin, but much initiative was left to local commanders. The forces were supported by Irish labor unions as well as by women's auxiliaries and by a boys' organization.[38]

The IRA began its campaign by boycotting, and later by murdering policemen. There were numerous killings of real or suspected informers. The revolutionaries organized an effective system of espionage that penetrated deep into the British administrative and police services. They also employed the "protection racket" for political purposes, and collected financial subscriptions from willing and unwilling people, either by appeals to patriotism or by threats of murder or destruction of property. In the cities the war often became an underground gang war, with killings and counter-killings, reprisals and counter-reprisals. In the countryside the insurgents organized "Flying Columns" that operated in bog or mountain country where communications were poor and pursuit difficult. The partisans laid ambushes, attacked police stations and other installations. They lived off the country and, when pressed, melted into the civilian population. The IRA virtually disrupted the British intelligence network; "Dublin Castle" lost control over many outlying areas.

From the purely military point of view, the Irish rebels were laboring under enormous disadvantages. The partisans could not rely on help from an outside army. The British therefore enjoyed great superiority in numbers and equipment. The guerrillas were worn out, and by the summer of 1921 the IRA's operational area was becoming ever more restricted. In many parts of the country guerrilla units dropped out of the fight and concluded local truces. Dry summer weather hardened the ground, and allowed military and police vehicles to drive round road blocks and trenches, or even to travel along hitherto impassable mountain roads. The long summer evenings gave the Flying Columns only a few hours of respite from attack.[39] Arms became scarce. Irish morale began to sag, and the Irish people as a whole became bitterly weary of the war. Had the British persisted, they

[38] For a general account, written from the Irish point of view, see Dorothy Macardle, *The Irish Republic: A Documented Chronicle of the Anglo-Irish Conflict and the Partitioning of Ireland, with a Detailed Account of the Period 1916-1923* (London, Victor Gollancz, 1937).

[39] Richard Bennett, *The Black and Tans* (London, Edward Hulton, 1959), pp. 208-9.

could have won. The rebels could have been immobilized by the systematic confiscation of motor transport, horses, and bicycles. Irish financial resources could have been disrupted by the closing of post offices and banks. Concerted pressure on the remaining gangs would have worn down all remaining resistance, especially if combined with pre-emptive arrests on a massive scale of potential sympathizers, and with the relocation of people in disaffected areas. The British would have had to pay a heavy price, however, for such a policy. They would have had to govern Ireland by means of a military regime. Political reconciliation would have been impossible. The executions of 1916, the introduction of conscription during the Great War, the activities of the Black and Tans, the British decision to partition Ireland into a predominantly Catholic south and a mainly Protestant north, did not permit the restoration of the status quo antebellum.

The Irish finally gained by political means what they had not been able to win by purely military expedients. The Irish nationalists set up a shadow government. In many cases they dispensed their own justice, raised their own taxes, dealt with a host of administrative problems, and thereby kept the political initiative. Britain was desperately war-weary, for the Great War had already taken an enormous toll in blood and treasure. Britain's imperial position was threatened as far afield as Egypt, Mesopotamia, and India. British troops were stationed in many parts of the world from Cologne to Constantinople, and the British had no stomach for further commitments. The British will to fight therefore was the first to give way. The British Labour movement as well as many Tories wanted peace in Ireland. The British war effort was impeded still further by trade union troubles in England itself.

The British imperial cause was also losing the battle for men's minds. The British, very unwisely, reinforced their Royal Irish Constabulary by ex-soldiers whose service experience, gained in the trenches, was quite inappropriate to the IRA's hit-and-run raids. The "Black and Tans," often under severe provocation, resorted to bloody reprisals. They were unfamiliar with conditions in the country. They could identify neither their friends nor their enemies, and would often raid the houses of people sympathetic to the British cause. They thereby acquired an undeserved reputation for limitless cruelty. Judged by the standards of totalitarian warfare, the British were mild enough: there were no mass executions of prisoners or of hostages and there were no concentration camps. But the Irish war, with its killings in back alleys and country lanes, was conducted under a blaze of newspaper publicity which suggested, quite mistakenly, that the whole country was aflame and that the whole country was wallowing in blood.[40]

The Irish managed their press relations with outstanding ability. They even laid on special tours for foreign journalists, known as "Irish Scenic Railway trips," and got their case widely accepted on the European continent, in America (where Irish emigrants furnished both moral and financial support), and in Britain itself. The bulk of British intellectuals opposed the war. Friends of Irish independence included socialists and pacifists, right-wing Catholics like G. K. Chesterton and Hilaire Belloc, professional soldiers, and Horatio Bottomley, a political mountebank and swindler. The Irish war itself became a bargaining counter in British politics, and in 1921 the British gave up the struggle. The strife-torn island was divided, and the southern portion at long last set out on an independent political career of its own.

The Irish revolutionaries had played their cards with much skill. But they could not make headway in northeast Ulster, the northern province of Ireland, where the majority of the population were Protestants, and where religion commonly helped to cement a curious form of protonationalism. The division between Unionists and Irish nationalists transcended class alignments. Most Catholics, of whom there were many (especially beyond the conurbation of Belfast), stood for a united Ireland. So did a minority of Protestants, including some great capitalists such as Lord Pirrie, who controlled the great shipyards of Harland and Wolff. But the Unionists formed the majority. They could rely on a broad social coalition. They derived support not only from factory owners, army officers, gentry, and farmers, but also from the

---

[40] The Irish casualties were estimated at only about 700 killed and 800 wounded. British casualties amounted to some 528 policemen and soldiers killed, and 1166 soldiers and policemen wounded.

great majority of Protestant working men who were fearful of Catholic competition for jobs.

The Irish civil war cannot be assessed simply in social terms; it must be seen against the background of a long, bloodstained history of plantations. Many Protestants were descended from Scottish and English settlers whose ancestors had dispossessed the indigenous Irish peasantry and gentry. Protestants feared that Home Rule would turn into "Rome Rule," with dire consequences for the Protestants' future. The Ulstermen were determined to maintain their connection with the United Kingdom, by force if necessary, and they knew how to organize.

In 1913, just before the outbreak of World War I, the British House of Commons passed a Home Rule bill that would have granted Ireland a limited form of autonomy but that would have included Ulster in a united Ireland. The Protestants in the northeast prepared to resist, and formed the Ulster Volunteers, resolved to set up a separate government in Belfast should the Home Rule bill become law. In many ways, therefore, the Ulstermen helped to pioneer the formation of modern private armies (such as the Jewish Haganah in Mandatory Palestine, and other equally combatworthy formations).

The Ulstermen had many supporters within the British army, including some of the most senior British officers. They proved as competent in the art of mobilizing public opinion as the Catholics. They obtained a great deal of backing in Great Britain and also in North America (especially in Canada). Many British professional soldiers volunteered to fight for Ulster's cause. The Ulster Volunteers were able to use local factories owned by wealthy Protestant sympathizers as bases for training and for supplies. The Ulstermen were even able to import goods through privately owned port facilities. Like their Catholic opponents, with whom they had much in common, the Ulstermen insisted on a high standard of efficiency. They were skilled at organizing ancillary services and at gun-running. Their staff arrangements included plans for disrupting the railways and telegraph lines. The Ulster Volunteers were in advance of their times by fully appreciating, before the First World War, the importance of mechanized transport, and they organized a

Motor Transport Corps of their own. Their planners fully understood the importance of guerrilla warfare. As one of their staff memoranda put it, the essential thing was to deceive the enemy and to hit him hard before he was ready.[41]

The outbreak of the First World War probably prevented civil conflict in Ireland as Irishmen of all faiths rallied against the Germans. After the end of the war, the Irish nationalists tried to include Ulster in their design for a united republic; but the Ulstermen were too well organized, and Ulster to this day remains part of the United Kingdom. Skill in organizing irregular operations, in other words, had no necessary connection with any particular orientation in politics. In many respects the southern military movement was indeed a mirror image of its opposite number in the north. Southern and northern Irish leaders were fully aware of the need for combining rural with city-born operations. The Irish, like the Moroccans, had some geographical space at their disposal; their operations were not confined to purely urban theaters of war.

Revolutionaries who fought only in cities suffered, however, from severe disabilities. The history of irregular war throughout the nineteenth and in the twentieth century offers not a single example of an urban insurrection that succeeded without widespread backing in the countryside. There are of course a few examples of city-born risings that had profound political consequences even though they turned out to be complete failures from the military standpoint. The Easter Rising in Dublin was a fiasco. But it turned into a political success because the British mishandled the situation. In South Africa, a nearly contemporary insurrection organized in 1922 by white miners on the Witwatersrand likewise turned into a military defeat but a political victory. The South African revolt was confined to a small socio-ethnic section. The skilled white workers took to arms in order to defend their standard of living against competition from lower-paid black workers. The insurgents, who drew their inspiration both from Marxist sources and from the militant nationalism of white Afrikaners, rallied

---

[41] A. T. Q. Stewart, *The Ulster Crisis* (London, Faber and Faber, 1967), p. 120.

behind the strangely compounded slogan "Workers of the World Unite and Fight for a White South Africa." The white miners were well armed. They organized their own commandos and seized much of the Rand. The Africans were thoroughly cowed and remained neutral. The South African army faced a difficult task, for many reservists, poverty-stricken Afrikaners from the backwoods, sympathized with the rebels. The South African government forces had to fight hard to suppress what had hitherto been the only great urban rising in sub-Saharan Africa. In the end the miners lost. They did, however, extract political benefits from their willingness to fight. In 1924 the existing South African government was voted out of office and was replaced by an alliance between Afrikaans-speaking farmers and white workers. The so-called Nationalist-Labour Pact granted special concessions to the white working men, and the European working class was successfully absorbed into the South African Establishment.

The Viennese workers who battled against Catholic conservatives in 1934 were not so fortunate. Though well organized, the Austrian Social Democrats suffered a smashing defeat for, like the Paris Communards, they lacked armed support outside the capital, and their social basis was relatively narrow. In this connection, the same lesson may be learned from the urban insurrections that occurred during World War II: that urban risings may be of major political significance but that they cannot possibly attain military success as long as the rebels are confined only to one great city.

From these unsuccessful urban insurrections, we turn to operations of a more variegated kind. The interwar period witnessed many instances of partisan warfare, some of them highly successful. In Palestine, for instance, the British mandatory power had to cope with an Arab rising directed primarily against Jewish immigration. The British put down the revolt by army and police formations, assisted by Jewish counterguerrilla squads familiar with the terrain, trained in night operations, and scarcely distinguishable in appearance from their opponents.[42] The Jews proved thereby that the counterguerrilla, as mobile, resolute, and ubiquitous as his

[42] See Leonard Oswald Mosley, *Gideon Goes to War* (New York, Scribner's, 1955), *passim*.

opponent, is worth more than the orthodox soldier when it comes to conducting anti-partisan operations.

4. Partisan Warfare since the Start of the Second World War

By the beginning of World War II, students of military affairs had a wide field from which to generalize on the subject of partisan warfare. Oddly enough, however, few defense experts showed much interest in such matters. In a world where regular forces were supplied with aircraft and tanks, motorized transport, radio sets, and self-propelled artillery, guerrilla operations generally seemed no more than anachronistic survivals.[43] The British, with their wide experience in South Africa, Ireland, and Palestine, had retained some inkling of the problem. Subsequently they became once more expert practitioners in the art of waging "small wars." The Americans had once led the world in the art of guerrilla warfare. The American War of Independence, the American Civil War, and American campaigns in the Philippines had all afforded some of the most splendid examples of successful partisan and counterinsurgency operations. By the beginning of the Second World War, however, these lessons had largely been forgotten; subsequent guerrilla operations like those against the Japanese in the Philippines had to be improvised from scratch. The Germans in the interwar years had acquired plenty of experience in irregular field operations as well as in street fighting: ex-Free Corps volunteers played a significant part in right-wing storm troop formations. But German nationalism was rarely intended as an exportable commodity. The Germans raised "special forces" for the *Wehrmacht*, but the wartime use of irregular units was confined above all to members of German minority groups in foreign countries. The famous German "Fifth Column" operated largely in immediate concert with the *Wehrmacht*. The smaller Eastern European countries all put their trust in outmoded conventional armies. Except in the case of

---

[43] Heilbrunn, *Warfare in the Enemy's Rear, passim.*

60

Switzerland, whose defenses were never tested, no European power prepared guerrilla operations in advance.

The sudden collapse of Britain's continental allies between 1939 and 1941, however, forced a new military policy on the occupied nations of Europe. Britain survived as an "unsinkable air-craft carrier," as a military base, and as a living inspiration to the forces of resistance. In Western Europe the will to hold out gradually revived, but Western Europe lacked suitable terrain for large-scale guerrilla units. The British therefore encouraged members of the resistance to concentrate on sabotage, on the gathering of intelligence, and on carrying out small coups. The Royal Air Force dropped instructors and liaison officers, as well as equipment and explosives. Large-scale guerrilla operations only began once the Allies had landed in Europe, commonly in areas where partisans could directly cooperate with Allied land forces. In the Soviet Union, partisan operations reached even larger proportions. The German army could not effectively control the whole of the vast country. Swamps, forests, and sometimes mountain country offered an excellent terrain. The Communist Party and the NKVD echelons often remained in existence in areas under German rule, and often provided cadres for resistance. The Nazis alienated the bulk of the population by their insane atrocities. They would not rebuild an independent peasantry by redistributing socialized land. In short, they had nothing to offer but terror. The Russian guerrillas could never be mopped up, though their ability to interfere with German military operations remained strictly limited. It was the Soviet armies which bore the brunt of the battle. Nor did the partisans ever develop into a truly effective independent political force. The communists always struggled hard to keep these multifarious units under effective political and military control and to prevent deviationism.

In Poland there was likewise a widespread underground movement which comprised possibly a larger percentage of the population than in any other country. By 1944 well over half a million people were supporting the various underground armies of differing political complexions, with the vast majority backing the exiled government in London. The Poles were seriously hampered by the topography of their country as well as by divided counsel. They could not seriously shake the German hold on their country nor effectively disrupt German communications. But the people of Poland were the most resolute urban insurrectionaries of occupied Europe.

The first to fight the Germans in the streets were the Jews of Warsaw. These few remaining survivors of the Nazi terror embarked on a desperate and forlorn venture, seeking not victory nor the rhetoric of victory, but death. Militarily, the significance of the Ghetto rising was nil; psychologically, its impact on the Jewish people was tremendous. Later on, in 1944, the population of Warsaw at large took to arms against the German occupying power. The Poles thereby had the distinction of staging the only major urban rising that broke out in Nazi-occupied Europe without support from Allied armies. The Red Army did not move. The Polish rebels were destroyed, and the remnants of the pro-London resistance movement were later liquidated by Soviet forces. But the legend lives on and continues to inspire Polish nationalists of the most varied political hues.

In Yugoslavia partisan warfare followed a somewhat different pattern. The Royal Yugoslav Army, like the Soviet armies, failed to prepare in advance for guerrilla warfare. The Yugoslavs made the additional mistake of not concentrating their resistance in the mountain redoubts of the south. Yugoslav resistance, therefore, quickly collapsed. General Mihailovich, commander of a motorized division, a nationalist, and, like De Gaulle, a longstanding advocate of mechanized warfare, continued resistance and built up a partisan movement. Mihailovich, however, unlike his communist competitors, lacked both revolutionary doctrine and an already existing underground movement on which he could count for propaganda, recruitment, and intelligence. His forces were based mainly in Serbia and were assigned fixed geographical areas. Without a strong, mobile reserve, Mihailovich meant to carry on the same kind of resistance as the French, to conduct harassing and sabotage operations. It was his hope to organize a general national rising once Allied troops should disembark on the Adriatic coast.

Mihailovich, however, met with effective competition from the Yugoslav communists, who at the outbreak of the war already possessed a centralized, well-disciplined party organization. The communists felt no concern about bloody German reprisals against the civilian population, as did Mihailovich. They succeeded in building up a widespread resistance movement that drew its main strength from the country's "peripheral" areas like Bosnia and Croatia. The communists stood for a Yugoslav form of federalism, a solution that made much more appeal to the masses than Mihailovich's militant Serbian nationalism. The communists successfully employed the strategy of a "united front." (Indeed the so-called Bihach Manifesto, issued in 1942 by the Anti-Fascist Council for the National Liberation of Yugoslavia, affirmed the inviolability of private property, and promised that no radical changes would be made in the social life of the people.) In Tito the guerrillas had an able leader, the only Balkan communist who succeeded in building up a big underground army during the war. Tito relied not only on territorial units, but also on organized mobile forces, available for deployment anywhere in the country. These units were stiffened with seasoned revolutionary fighters with experience in Spain and in other parts of the world. Tito successfully resisted a number of German attempts to annihilate the guerrillas by means of concentric drives. In 1944 he succeeded in obtaining a monopoly of Allied (largely British) underground support. His position was further strengthened when the Red Army helped to liberate the country in 1944, thereby disappointing Mihailovich's hopes for Western military intervention. The Yugoslav communists thus successfully established a revolutionary dictatorship, and Mihailovich, abandoned by the Western powers, died before a firing squad.

On the other side of the world, the invading Japanese army in China could likewise never smash the guerrillas, for numbers and space operated against the invaders. The Japanese, unlike Jewish counterguerrillas in Palestine, could not merge into the countryside. The Japanese usually defeated their enemies in set-piece battles. They were, however, unable to cope with a hostile population and the vast spaces of China. Whereas the Japanese were able to crush hostile guerrillas in Korea, they could not repeat this feat in China. The Chinese Communists, taught in the hard school of civil war against Chinese Nationalists, became masters in the art of guerrilla war. They evolved a complex doctrine of protracted war whereby the Communists would first confine themselves to the strategic defensive, then gradually reverse the balance, prepare for counterattack, and finally force the enemy to withdraw.

Mao Tse-tung, the greatest modern practitioner and theoretician of this type of warfare, gave Marxist strategy a new twist by reversing orthodox Marxist practice. Mao relied on the peasantry, the most "backward" section of the Chinese people, instead of on the urban proletariat favored by Marx and his Russian successors. Mao stressed the need for secure bases and for gaining the support of the masses. The people in a communist-dominated area must be organized into three groups. The bulk of the people would be grouped into self-defense units with limited military capacities. They would root out "reactionaries," give general political support to the fighting forces and supply reserves. Guerrillas would attack the enemy in certain well-defined areas. Regulars would engage in more ambitious operations. Mao insisted on aggressive tactics. Partisans were enjoined to gain the sympathy of the people, to abstain from stealing food or from molesting women, and finally to convert the masses to their doctrine. The guerrilla's strength depended on his ability to operate behind the enemy's rear as well as his front line. This was possible only if the bands were able to move among the population like fish in the water.[44]

Up to this point, Mao Tse-tung's doctrines differed little from those of Lawrence of Arabia. The Chinese Communists, however, went much farther both in the military and in the political sphere than the British guerrilla leader. Lawrence, an impulsive and wayward man, was inclined to underestimate the decisive role played by regular British forces in defeating the Turks; and he tended to overestimate the importance of guerrillas acting on their own. Mao Tse-tung did not fall into the same trap. Mao conceived of guerrilla forces warfare as passing through a series of merging phases. First of all the partisans would organize and consolidate regional bases, an operation that obviously required a great deal of physical space and was difficult to carry out in a small country. After

---

[44]Mao Tse-tung, *Guerrilla Warfare, passim.*

organizing and consolidating their stronghold, they would convert the population to their cause. Even bandits might make acceptable recruits if properly indoctrinated. Military operations in this stage would be limited to small-scale actions, and the enemy would retain the strategic offensive. In the second phase the liberated areas would be expanded. Partisans would ambush weak columns, capture enemy arms, and improve the guerrillas' fighting potential. (This stage, roughly speaking, corresponded to the one reached by the IRA in the Irish "national" war.)

The communists made vast improvements over the methods used by the Irish and the Moroccans. Mao Tse-tung had infinitely more space at his disposal than Michael Collins or Abd-el-Krim. He could also draw on infinitely greater reserves of manpower. Mao therefore taught that in the third stage the guerrillas must transform a significant percentage of their forces into an orthodox army, capable of fighting conventional battles. This doctrine was reflected in his military organization. Mao argued, like Lawrence, that guerrillas must not in the first place allow themselves to be tied down by a big administrative "tail"; they must capture arms from the enemy and use the opposing commissariat as their source of supply.

On the lowest level guerrilla forces would be grouped into small units from platoon to company size. Then battalions of two to four companies would be formed. Next came the guerrilla regiment, which would be under severer discipline than the battalion. If manpower and arms were available, regiments would be grouped into brigades, which would be capable of large-scale engagements. At all times, however, these regular forces would continue to be supported by guerrilla units, trained to strike quickly, to disperse without delay, and to provide adequate intelligence to the regular armies. The last stages of the war might be interrupted by negotiations undertaken for the dual purpose of gaining time, buttressing new positions and frustrating the enemy. In the final stage the enemy, worn down and demoralized, would collapse before the momentum of the revolutionary masses.

Mao Tse-tung's political scheme in some ways corresponded to the military doctrine of merging phases. Mao, like Lenin, conceived of revolutionary politics as a series of accelerating struggles to wipe out the class enemy and create a totalitarian state resting on the dictatorship of the chosen revolutionary vanguard. Mao greatly expanded his movement by fighting anti-Japanese campaigns in which patriots from all social classes participated. But Mao, unlike Collins or Abd-el-Kader, was not content with a national war of liberation. War itself was conceived as a means of seizing and sustaining power. National wars were to culminate in revolution that would result in the liquidation of both the urban bourgeoisie and the rural gentry. The revolutionary government would in turn socialize the means of production and would extend the control of the communist vanguard to all aspects of social existence, molding both the nation's thought and its social structure according to a new pattern. Under the new dispensation the revolutionary functionary and the revolutionary theoretician would become the new depositories of power; their influence would be ideological as much as political. The movement therefore made a tremendous appeal to militant intellectuals, and propaganda came to play a vital part in communist military activities. Every independent guerrilla company was supplied with its own political officer and a mobile propaganda unit. Indoctrination with a revolutionary, "future-directed" creed therefore came to play an infinitely more important role in warfare than it had in most previous partisan campaigns.

The two world wars, fought for the purpose of ending all wars, failed to bring peace. Instead they created a military twilight world where there was neither peace nor war, where all lived in dread of the Armageddon to come, and where even the soldiers became unsure of how Armageddon was to be fought. The super-powers made costly preparations for nuclear struggles on a vast scale. But except for the Korean War, few great conventional armies ever became locked in battle. There were conflicts of the conventional kind in the Near East and elsewhere; but at the same time guerrillas acquired increasing importance, especially when they were backed by outside powers. Guerrilla operations and political gangsterism in some ways developed into a new kind of "limited" warfare; in fact they often became a substitute for all-out clashes between communist states and Western powers. Revolutionary warfare became "total," affecting every class of the population involved; yet the military means involved remained limited in nature.

Space forbids a complete résumé of all these numerous struggles, which indeed parallel much of contemporary history in the Afro-Asian world. The various guerrilla combats nevertheless may be divided into several clearly defined categories. The most obvious distinction is that between guerrilla movements that succeeded and those that failed. The number of failures is large, and should dispel the assumption — now widely held–that popular struggles are bound to succeed in the end. There have been no successful guerrilla movements against communist governments, however wide the rebels' popular backing. The combination of mass terror, unrestrained by an instructed popular opinion or by foreign intervention, and of a well-disciplined, militant party with branches in the remotest villages, supported by the full power of a totalitarian state, has successfully coped with any attempts at overthrowing communist states. For the present, changes within the communist power structure are likely to come from within rather than from without the party cadres.

Western powers too, one might add, have shown themselves capable of using terror. In 1947 the French, for instance, utterly destroyed a native rising in Madagascar. There was much bloodshed, but the Western world took little notice. Madagascar was remote from the main centers of world conflict and from the attention of the world press, now an important factor in the Western world. French anti-colonialists were preoccupied with the war in Indochina, and the United States was too busy with the opening campaigns of the Cold War and with the problem of setting Europe on its feet again.[45] The use of terror on its own, however, has been apt to yield diminishing dividends. Terror can buy time; it cannot serve as a substitute for a political program. The French subsequently granted independence to Madagascar, and Franco-Malagasy relations have since been marked by a surprising degree of cordiality. The Soviets still face the problem of how to cope with Polish, Hungarian, Czech, and other forms of national communism. Their

[45] Brian Crozier, *The Rebels: A Study of Post-War Insurrections* (London, Chatto and Windus, 1960), pp. 199-201.

troubles with the People's Republic of China have increased. But militarily, the post-Stalinist empire in Eastern Europe is now more powerful than ever before. There is no likelihood of effective opposition through guerrilla activity, while peaceful resistance has not seriously diverted the Soviets from their path.

Communists in the postwar world have, on the whole, been more successful in suppressing revolts than in seizing power by means of armed rebellions. The Red Army successfully wiped out anti-Soviet partisans in the Ukraine after the Second World War. The Russians smashed the Hungarian nationalist rising of 1956 within a remarkably short space of time. The Chinese Communists successfully overran Tibet and systematically liquidated the local opposition.

But communists were much less successful in countries that were removed from the physical grip of Soviet and Chinese regular forces. In places as far afield as Greece, Malaya, and the Philippines, communist partisans attempted to establish revolutionary dictatorships. Yet none of these efforts succeeded. In Malaya and the Philippines, communist guerrillas were exposed to the dual threat of sea power and social reform. The centers of rebellion were geographically isolated and could not be effectively supported from privileged sanctuaries outside.

The communists in Malaya drew their strength almost exclusively from one ethnic community only—the Chinese— and failed to make any headway among the Malay people. They alienated the population by slashing rubber trees, by burning buses and plantation buildings, and by extorting food supplies. In the end, therefore, the British came out on top.

The British fought their war in a highly intelligent fashion. Unlike the French in Algeria, they would not condone torture, but emphasized the need for capturing terrorists alive by providing them with an incentive to surrender, be it money, protection, or even the allocation of a house. After many initial mistakes, the British came to understand that army successes calculated in terms of "kills" were less important than psychological successes, whether among the partisans or the population at large. The authorities successfully employed former terrorists to lecture to villagers. The British also had a clear grasp of police work. Policemen usually have a better chance of getting to know their "manor" than soldiers on limited tours of duty. Policemen were taught how to gather intelligence, and they concentrated on bringing criminals to justice rather than on eliminating terrorists. There were, of course, many errors. There was hesitation in the use of emergency measures and delay in getting military reinforcements. Nor were police and civil service appointments always geared to the emergency. But the British nevertheless had a chance to redeem these mistakes. They resettled threatened peasants in protected villages. They gained the sympathy of the population by various political and economic reforms and, above all, by the promise of effective independence. They lured the enemy into baited "killing grounds," making good use of small, mobile jungle units supported by helicopters. In this kind of warfare, artillery proved expensive and relatively ineffective. Tanks were useless, though armored cars did valuable escort duty. The air force provided flexibility and logistic support. Airmen did a useful job also in liaison work and in psychological warfare operations in which the British excelled.

The key to success in these operations lay not simply in machine power, but in effective planning, in the human factor, in the Britons' ability to find and establish balance between offensive and defensive operations. The British, so to speak, learned how to use both the buckler and the sword. Above all, the British helped to pioneer the technique of resettling scattered farmers in defensible villages. In doing so, they took account not merely of military considerations. They also endeavored to create balanced communities, and they tried to move people with the least possible disruption of their lives. Peasants grouped in villages can more easily be provided with schools, agricultural services, and medical clinics than tillers who live in scattered little homesteads dispersed over vast areas. The relocation of villages thus became in itself an instrument both of counterinsurgency warfare and of social revolution. Without realizing it, the British in certain respects reapplied some of the principles concerning colonial warfare elaborated two generations earlier by Gallieni and his contemporaries in the French army, men who might be described as military reformists. (Similar methods were subsequently applied by the Portuguese army in Angola against African partisans. The Portuguese now attempt to turn their colonial army into an instrument of social revolution in the countryside. The future of their rule in Angola will hinge on the success or failure of this design.)

In the Philippines communist forces known as the "Huks" or Hukbalahap (People's Anti-Japanese Resistance Army) staged another insurrection. The Huks struck out against a corrupt government and against landlordism, but again the rebels failed to make serious headway. Combined pressure from counterguerrilla forces, backed by land reform and other social improvements initiated by Ramon Magsaysay (Defense Minister and later President), effectively put down the rising. Magsaysay created an efficient constabulary, talked captured communists into supporting him, trained dogs to hunt Huk units, and finally stamped out the rebellion by an outstanding instance of "enlightened repression."[46]

In Greece communist guerrillas were able to rely on land-based support from communist-dominated Albania and Yugoslavia. The Greek guerrillas, however, made the mistake of alienating many peasants by large-scale food requisitions and other even more onerous impositions. In 1948 they lost political support from Yugoslavia when Tito broke with Stalin. In addition they became too dependent on their base areas, especially the northern region of Vitsi and Grammos on the borders with Yugoslavia and Albania. This base had to be defended permanently. In 1949 they were compelled to give battle in orthodox fashion, for which they had neither the training nor the equipment. Their positions were overrun, and the war was over.[47]

On the other hand, communist guerrilla forces gained a brilliant victory against the French in what used to be Indochina. The Viet Minh profited from Mao Tse-tung's

[46] See Napoleon D. Valeriano and Charles T. R. Bohannan, *Counter-Guerrilla Operations: The Philippine Experience* (New York, Frederick A. Praeger, 1962), *passim*.

[47] Otto Heilbrunn, *Partisan Warfare* (New York, Frederick A. Praeger, 1962), pp. 46-47.

experience, though they did not follow the Chinese precedent in all respects. The communist-directed National Unity Front was, in Viet Minh parlance, an alliance between the workers and the peasants under the leadership of the working class. According to General Giap, the most outstanding of Viet Minh soldiers, the Front originally underestimated the importance of the peasant question, but subsequently corrected this error.[48] The communists reduced land rents and interest rates. Communal land rights and rice fields were more evenly distributed as many private owners lost their holdings. The communists for a while differentiated between so-called patriotic and reactionary members of the landlord class, and by this means they were able to gain considerable popular support for a time. The French, already exhausted by a world war and the German occupation, had to supply an army fighting half-way round the world. The guerrillas, on the other hand, imported weapons and other goods from nearby China, and they also captured much war material from the French. From the military point of view, Giap saw the destruction of the enemy's manpower as his chief goal, and he successfully stepped up the struggle from minor guerrilla actions to big battles.

From 1948 the communists fought engagements with one or more battalions. The guerrillas' position improved further beginning in 1950 when the Chinese communists appeared on the border. The Viet Minh overran several strategic frontier forts. Supplies became assured, and the partisans were able to send whole regiments and even larger formations into the fray. The Viet Minh thus launched campaigns on a much larger scale. They maintained a successful balance between partisan and conventional operations, and created a situation where "free zones" became interlaced with enemy-held areas. In hostile regions the insurgents likewise built up guerrilla zones and guerrilla bases, which expanded as the war progressed.

The French for their part made various mistakes. They overextended their forces. They could not appeal to the mass of the people. They also had great difficulties in freeing

---

[48] "Giap on Guerrilla Warfare," in *Insurgency and Counterinsurgency: An Anthology*, Richard M. Leighton and Ralph Sanders, eds. (Industrial College of the Armed Forces, Washington, D.C., 1962), pp. 139-48.

themselves from the shackles of conventional logistics. Motor trucks and motorized infantry could not move through trackless jungle, whereas Viet Minh carriers managed to negotiate the most difficult country imaginable, and foot-slogging Viet Minh fighting squads achieved astonishing mobility. The French tried to fight too far from their bases. Strategically audacious, their tactics were marked by road-bound movements and conventional hedgehog defense. All too often they would strike deep into enemy country without adequately safeguarding their own lines of communication and supply.[49] The French commanders in Indochina indeed committed many of the mistakes made by Napoleon's generals in Spain. They neglected the essential principle that effective counterguerrilla operations depend on a combination of close territorial control with effective striking forces. In the end their grip weakened in a disastrous fashion, and they began to suffer defeats in major as well as minor battles. The communists, for their part, mastered the art of positional as well as of mobile warfare, and in 1954 they brought off a spectacular victory at Dien Bien Phu. Dien Bien Phu did not by any means knock out the French army, but the French were tired of fighting a desperately bloody and expensive war on the other side of the world, and in 1954 they gave up the struggle.

The criterion of success or failure seems the most obvious basis for the classification of guerrilla warfare. Partisan movements may be distinguished also, however, according to the goals they pursue. In the postwar world the old pattern of "national" warfare, directed simply at expelling an alien ruler, generally gave way to social struggles that aimed at a revolutionary transformation of power and at the redistribution of property. The major exceptions are to be found in the eastern Mediterranean, where several "national" movements gained local supremacy. In Cyprus, for instance, EOKA, a militant Greek organization, fought to expel the British and to unite the island with Greece. Colonel Grivas, the Greek leader, adopted policies and tactics that stand comparison with those of Michael Collins; and from the purely military point of view his movement was not

---

[49]Peter Paret and John W. Shy, *Guerrillas in the 1960's* (New York, Frederick A. Praeger, 1962), pp. 41-42.

particularly successful. Grivas met with opposition not merely from the British, but also from the Turkish minority on the island, which played a role comparable in certain respects to that of the loyalist Ulstermen in Ireland. The British very nearly succeeded in snuffing out EOKA, but they failed to consolidate their political position. The war ended with a compromise that gave Cyprus independence but eschewed *enosis* (union with Greece).

In the Suez Canal Zone Egyptian guerrilla activities, directed by the Egyptian government, won unconditional success. The British became convinced that final withdrawal was inevitable and pulled out. Cypriots and Egyptians alike benefited from British war-weariness, from expert publicity, from British unwillingness to employ mass terrorism, and from political support within Great Britain itself. The British had been ruthless enough during the Second World War when they put down a nationalist and anti-British conspiracy in Iraq without giving a thought to the morals of the case. But on this occasion Britain's national existence had seemed at stake, and the rebels had been identified with the Nazi enemy. After 1945 Britain's wartime cohesion was a thing of the past, and, as formerly in Ireland, the British in Cyprus and Egypt were defeated by their conscience as much as by enemy action.

In Palestine the British became involved in a complex triangular battle against the Jews on the one hand and the Arabs on the other. The Jewish fighting organizations were themselves divided into Haganah, the main underground army, the Irgun Zvai Leumi, and the Stern Gang, militant organizations that sometimes were opposed and sometimes tolerated by the main bulk of the settlers. The Jews as a whole stood both for a nationalistic and for what might be called a civilizational creed. They looked to a Jewish homeland, where mass immigration would renew their ancient state. The new Israel would not only rival the splendors of ancient Zion, but would also form a cultural focus for world Jewry, as well as a social laboratory for the Middle East. The British had no answer to militant ideologies of this kind. They made a well-meant but unconvincing effort to invent a "Palestinian" nationality that would transcend the division between Jew and Arab. But such a concept had

73

no chance against the militancy of a national-religious creed, preaching secular redemption. The Jews had obtained much military experience in many parts of the world. Unlike most colonial subjects, they were also the equals of their rulers in the technological sphere. The Jews indeed considered themselves to be technically better qualified to run the state machinery than the British. In some ways like the Irish, the Jews successfully created the elements of a "proto-state" under the Mandatory government itself.

Jewish terrorism played an important, though not a decisive, part in terminating the British mandate. The Jewish fighting groups enjoyed the advantage of passive support from the Jewish civilian population. They knew how to enforce proper timing. They had an excellent intelligence system, and they commanded an up-to-date technology. Armed action by itself could not, however, have succeeded in driving the British out of Palestine. The partisans could not bring the transport system to a standstill. The British perfected curfews and cordons. They traced arms caches by means of mine detectors. They successfully employed police dogs.[50] But in the end the British left because they felt that the Mandate no longer paid. Mounting costs might have been borne, bomb attacks might have been withstood, and American pressure resisted, if the British retention of Palestine had been essential to Britain's military security or to her economic survival. Neither of these conditions applied, however, and the British pulled out.

On the very opposite end of the spectrum stood African risings like the Mau Mau rebellion in Kenya. The causes of the Mau Mau insurrection are too complex to be easily summarized. Suffice it to say that the Kikuyu tribe had suffered extensive disruption and profound frustration. The Kikuyu reserves had become incapable of yielding a satisfactory livelihood to an expanding population. The Kikuyu claimed extensive land areas alienated to European settlers, who had developed modern farms in the bush but whose prosperity and privileges excited the anger of the landless. Kenya moreover lacked secondary industries. There were simply not enough jobs to go around; and the Kikuyu, who

[50]R. D. Wilson, *Cordon and Search: With 6th Airborne Division in Palestine* (Aldershot [Eng.], Gale and Polden, 1949), *passim*.

contained a higher percentage of educated and partly Europeanized people than any other Kenyan tribe, became increasingly resentful and rebellious. Many Kikuyu began to advocate the expulsion of European farmers. Many turned against Christianity and called for the restoration of ancient customs like female circumcision. The Kikuyu women especially opposed government-sponsored soil conservation programs. They argued that the hard work entailed in the digging of contour ridges and effecting similar improvements would be more profitably spent in the cultivation of their ancestral acres in the accustomed manner.

After a lengthy period of unrest, and after many missed opportunities on the government's side, the Kikuyu went on the warpath, turning not only against the Europeans, but also against the "loyalists" of their own race, with the result that the rising to some extent became a Kikuyu civil war between those who had land and those who had none. Gang fighting broke out in city and country alike, and the rebels combined all kinds of magical practices with the more humdrum features of partisan warfare. The British responded to terror by massive arrests, by large-scale resettlement and re-indoctrination programs. But above all, the rulers elaborated older methods of infiltration, used earlier, but to a much lesser extent against Jewish and Arab guerrillas in Palestine and against communist partisans in the Malayan jungle. The British formed pseudo-gangs, made up of captured and converted terrorists, led by European commanders. The pseudo-gangs infiltrated into genuine Kikuyu combat groups, and in the end the rising was successfully smashed.[51]

"Backward-looking" warfare of this kind was not confined to Kenya alone. Decolonization in the Congo led to a breakdown of the administration, to inflation, and to a wide measure of economic distress. The "revolution of rising expectations" and the disappointments of decolonization merged with more ancient traditions of rural radicalism, with local tribal or regional grievances, and with Messianic hopes for a better future. In 1964 widespread risings broke out in the east and north of the country, as well as in the Kwilu province of the center. The rebels included diverse social

[51] See for instance, Ian Henderson, with Philip Goodhart, *Manhunt in Kenya* (Garden City, N.Y., Doubleday and Co., 1958), *passim*.

groups — disaffected politicians, discontented villagers, unemployed urban youths, as well as street-corner thugs. They concentrated their propaganda against the Congolese Africans known as *les profiteurs du régime*, the new *bourgeoisie bureaucratique,* that is to say, the black politicians, the civil servants, the soldiers and police officers who seemed to have stepped into the Belgians' shoes. The insurgents called for a "Second Independence," a Messianic kingdom where all wrongs would be righted, where official exactions would be ended, and where prosperity would reign supreme.

The Congolese rebels were divided by ethnic quarrels, and by differences of leadership and strategy. They did, however, successfully employ guerrilla tactics for a time. Their fighting methods blended the old with the new, the use of poisoned arrows with the employment of modern weapons. Marxism mingled with magic. Rebel soldiers came to believe on the one hand that American and Belgian capitalists had invaded the Congo to exploit the people, and on the other that enemy bullets could be rendered harmless by occult means. In certain instances the rebels carried out large-scale massacres of those educated Africans on whose shoulders the construction of a modern state would have to rest. And everywhere the insurgents proved incapable of coping with the problems of urban governance or of economic reconstruction.

The new variety of what might be called "bush Marxism" differed from many other rural insurrectionary movements in that the discontented villagers were not landless proletarians. Neither did they come from regions where there was exceptional pressure on the available acreage, or where the poor were exploited by rich landlords. These rebels still had a foothold in the traditional economy. They likewise often looked to an idealized past, which they were apt to confuse with a splendid future. Millenarian expectations in the civil field found their counterpart in the military sphere. The rebels widely believed that magic precautions were bound to give them victory against all comers. (In this respect they resembled earlier generations of black resistance fighters, such as the participants in the Maji-Maji rebellion in former German East Africa, 1905-1907.)

The flight into superstition had certain short-term advantages for guerrilla fighters. It fortified their morale; it rendered extra impetus to the charges of armed tribesmen; it often terrified government troops. In the long run, however, magic turned out to be a treacherous ally. The rebels could not easily transcend their tribal affiliations: militarily, they might meet their match when they clashed with rival bands who were convinced of the superiority of their own witch doctors. Moreover, magic was useless against Europeans, who had no belief in a magic creed in the first place. Warriors who hold themselves to be invulnerable are adjusted only to the simple shock tactics of a preindustrial age. They will charge bravely, but they cannot cope with concealed machine gunners.[52] Such victories as were gained by white mercenaries over indigenous Congolese did not derive so much from personal courage or stamina, qualities in which black warriors are in no wise inferior to white soldiers. The Europeans were successful because they were better organized and better led, because they were technically more competent, and also because they refused to be intimidated by magical beliefs that terrified more superstitious fighting men.

[52] African guerrilla leaders are themselves acutely aware of this difficulty. The left wing Movimento Popular de Libertação de Angola, which now fights the Portuguese, thus accuses the rival partisan organization, known as União das Populacoes de Angola, of wishing to massacre all educated Africans, as well as the whites and the mulattos, of encouraging Africans to smoke hashish, of manufacturing "fetishes" designed to render black men invulnerable to bullets, and of promoting tribalism. The use of magic has allegedly occasioned the death of thousands of guerrilla fighters by encouraging warriors to launch futile mass attacks. See Movimento Popular de Libertação de Angola, *Libération des Colonies Portugaises: Angola* (Algiers, Presses de l'I.P.P., 1969), pp. 98, 110.

5. The Place of Partisan Warfare in History

Can anything be learned from this array of revolutionary wars and guerrilla actions? At first sight all these operations seem to have nothing in common. The art of small wars is as old as the history of warfare itself. The technique of partisan warfare cannot be labeled either reactionary or progressive. It is based essentially on the precepts of common sense, and requires no particular mystique for its elucidation. Revolutionary struggles had been waged untold centuries before Mao Tse-tung and other modern practitioners of this form of combat. "Bourgeois" nationalists, revolutionary socialists, clerically-minded peasants, and secular-minded peasants have all, at some time or another, excelled in the guerrilla's craft. Some revolutionaries have sought to put their trust in a "future-directed" program; others have tried to restore the past. Some, like the FLN and the Mau Mau, have used terror and torture as a matter of policy; others, like the Irgun Zvai Leumi, have been relatively restrained in their methods. Swamps, jungles, and inaccessible mountain country have traditionally provided the guerrillas' most favorable habitat; yet gangs have also operated successfully in cities.

Methods of suppressing partisans have also varied in the extreme. The Chinese in Tibet and the Russians in Hungary won by massive terror; yet frightfulness failed to yield results when employed by the Germans against Russian and Yugoslav partisans. The more diplomatic methods used by the British, restrained as they were in most instances by a humanitarian tradition, by Parliamentary inquiries and debates, by newspaper publicity, and generally by the continued operation of civilian courts, have also known their victories and their defeats. In Malaya the British introduced social and political reforms to gain the support of the people. Yet in Cyprus the British came very near to victory without having converted the Greek-speaking Cypriots to their cause. The successes won by revolutionary guerrilla campaigns in the postwar period can in fact easily be overestimated.

Victories in China, in North Vietnam, and in Cuba, for instance, are balanced by an impressive list of failures in Malaya and the Philippines, in Kenya and in Angola (where the Portuguese have to operate against guerrillas operating from "privileged sanctuaries abroad"). In Algeria the French finally withdrew for political and financial reasons, but they had not in any sense suffered a military defeat.

Yet historians can arrive at a few tentative generalizations. From the technical point of view, partisan operations on their own remain subject to severe limitations. They tend to be at their most effective when carried out in direct concert with regular forces, as, for instance, during the Peninsular War. For all the glamour with which partisan warfare has been endowed by rhetoricians, it always exacts a grim price from all the combatants, especially from the side that resists the invader. During the eighteenth century Spain and its Latin American colonies alike had steadily increased in wealth and prosperity. The partisan campaign against Napoleon had a disastrous effect on the economy of the Iberian Peninsula. The long-drawn-out war of independence waged by the Spanish American colonies against the motherland, a conflict set off in the first instance by Napoleon's invasion of Spain, set back the progress of Latin America for untold decades. The cost of partisan warfare moreover cannot be assessed merely in terms of limbs shattered and lives lost. From the standpoint of a statistician, a guerrilla operation may be much less destructive than an air raid or a rocket attack. But its moral and psychological effects are likely to be greater. An air raid has an impersonal quality about it. Sirens wail; planes drone overhead; seachlights pierce the sky; flak thunders; bombs whistle; walls shake; houses collapse. But no one knows the name of the pilot who drops the blockbusters. An air raid in some ways appears like a catastrophe of nature. Guerrilla warfare, on the other hand, entails personal violence. Partisan operations usually entail reprisals; reprisals lead to counterreprisals. Terror becomes commonplace until it takes a Goya to paint *Los Desastres de la Guerra*. Guerrilla warfare thus leaves a heritage of hate that may endure for generations, and may continue when the memories of conventional war have grown dim.

As regards the more technical side of guerrilla warfare,

historians can likewise discern certain regular patterns. Partisans require a geographical base. This is best established in regions with a difficult terrain, in rugged mountain country, in swamp and jungle land. But guerrillas also need a social environment conducive to unrest. Guerrillas are likely to make most progress in countries where the administration is weak, or where there has been a breakdown, or at any rate a partial breakdown, of the machinery for law enforcement. Such a collapse may come about in various ways. Foreign invasion may destroy the existing state machinery. The police forces may become subverted by infiltration. They may be weakened by the rulers' unwillingness to make adequate use of the coercive machinery at their disposal. Such unwillingness, whether derived from fear or from legal formalism, is liable to sap the morale of the police, and provide a moral dividend to the revolutionary. As Aristotle wrote more than two thousand years ago:

> In all well-attempered governments there is nothing which should be more jealously maintained than the spirit of obedience to law, more especially in small matters; for transgression creeps in unperceived and at last ruins the state, just as the constant recurrence of small expenses in time eats up a fortune. The expense does not take place all at once, and therefore is not observed; the mind is deceived, as in the fallacy which says that "if each part is little, then the whole is little." And this is true in one way, but not in another, for the whole and the all are not little, although they are made up of littles.[53]

Guerrilla movements can derive valuable support from sympathizers in cities. But urban risings such as those staged by the Paris Communards in 1871, by the white workers of Johannesburg in 1922, or by the Viennese Social Democrats in 1934, can never succeed without support in the country at large. Neither can urban warfare of the gangster variety destroy a state unless the rebels have the mass of the population behind them, and unless they can rely on at least the passive support of the regular armed forces.

Many political theoreticians have come to disagree with

[53]*The Student's Oxford Aristotle;* Vol. VI, *Politics and Poetics,* trans. into English under the editorship of W. D. Ross . . . (London, Oxford University Press, 1942), p. 1307b.

this assessment, and urban guerrilla warfare is being widely praised as a new form of insurrectionary action. Urban guerrilla warfare, in present-day revolutionary terminology, comprises many different activities, ranging from mass demonstrations to sabotage and political assassinations. Many advocates of urban guerrilla warfare moreover put special trust in an armed alliance between marginal intellectuals and marginal men of the slums. They overlook, however, the extreme difficulties of enforcing discipline among two groups which, by their very nature, resist discipline in its various forms. During the Spanish Civil War volunteers from many parts of Europe and America joined the International Brigades. These became élite units, capable of tackling the most difficult military tasks and willing to sustain terrific casualty rates without flinching. The radical movements that developed in Europe and in the United States during the late 1960s did not succeed in creating comparable bodies. Western European or American students may condemn Ian Smith and his fellow-fascists. But they do not travel to Southern Africa to fight against the Rhodesian Light Infantry in the bush. The failure of the new radicalism to create the counterpart of the Lincoln Brigade or the Attlee Brigade is by no means fortuitous. Military organization requires planning, discipline, and respect for leadership. These do not go well with a cult of Bohemian libertinage, romantic rhetoric, or a publicity-conscious cult of self-fulfillment.

Urban guerrillas have other problems of a more practical kind. What is possibly an over-cautious assessment derives from Che Guevara, who considered that guerrillas in built-up areas should always act under the direct command of superiors outside the city. Town-bred partisan bands should be small; they should not act independently, but should merely carry out their allotted share in a wider strategic plan.

This is important because the suburban guerrilla is working in an exceptionally unfavorable terrain, where the risks and consequences of exposure are tremendous. There is only little distance between the guerrilla's point of action and his refuge, so night action must predominate. He does not emerge into the open until the insurgents besiege the city.[54]

[54]Ernesto Guevara, *Che Guevara on Guerrilla Warfare* (New York, Frederick A. Praeger, 1961), p. 28.

Guevara is essentially correct, even though he perhaps underestimates the military potential of modern megalopolis. The rise of great conurbations, the development of an affluent working class and of a relatively well-to-do intelligentsia able to buy motor cars, trucks, and walkie-talkie sets has made the terrorist's task easier in certain respects. A modern industrial city contains large numbers of technicians and do-it-yourself amateurs, who can service complicated weapons, repair radios, and even produce home-made automatic guns and similar implements of war. Gasoline is cheap and easily available; so are a great variety of chemicals. Modern means of communication make the mobilization of huge crowds for the purpose of demonstrations a simple matter. The television camera and other means of publicity drawn from the armory of entertainers, advertisers, and clerics facilitate the task of making propaganda. The old-fashioned European city rebel of the past thought like an infantryman and fought like an infantryman. The modern urban guerrilla may, however, take a leaf from the book of the gangster. The modern bandit has adapted himself to an age of motorization. He can escape swiftly in his automobile. He has an extensive amount of space in which he can operate. His activities are harder to check in many ways than those of the criminal living in the pre-automobile age because the policeman in a car does not know his beat as well as his colleague on foot. Urban guerrilla warfare still looks for its Guderian, who will mechanize big-city partisan warfare by the use of motorized demolition squads and assault units concealed in delivery vans, repair trucks, and similar vehicles that can merge into ordinary traffic at night.

Modern cities depend on certain essential services such as water and electricity supplies. A well-trained, well-disciplined guerrilla unit might conceivably reduce a city to temporary havoc by striking at the right time in the right places. In communities like Singapore and Hong Kong, where the population is confined largely within the boundaries of a single city, sabotage linked to civil disobedience might be extremely effective. It is therefore essential for communities threatened with urban guerrilla warfare to protect workers in essential services and their families, and to plan relief measures before a community has actually been assaulted.

Urban guerrilla warfare is nevertheless subject to severe limitations. In large countries with extensive industrial resources, the economic and political effects of disorganizing a city quarter or even a whole city will not be permanent. Stricken areas can quickly be helped by areas that have remained unscathed. Attacks on essential services or on enterprises that provide people with their livelihood alienate the mass of the population. Hence the guerrillas soon face betrayal and liquidation. Townsmen moreover are a hardy breed no matter what their nationality. In countries as far afield as Great Britain and Poland, Germany and Japan, even the most heavily bombed towns showed the most amazing resilience during the Second World War. The authorities always managed to restore essential services with surprising speed after the most devastating air raids.

A "first-strike" capacity is not therefore sufficient. The urban guerrilla must follow up his initial successes by further action in order to keep his quarry off-balance. At this point he will meet his greatest difficulty. Even determined and ruthless urban guerrillas, such as the OAS (*Organisation de l'Armée Secrète*), the armed underground force of the French settlers in Algeria, never succeeded in forcing its will upon the country despite the fact that the OAS had some support from the French army, at least at certain times and in certain places. The settlers were mainly an urban group, who numbered only some ten percent of Algeria's population. They had no support among the mass of Muslims. The OAS had little power outside the towns. The OAS could control the bulk of the Europeans, but the settlers' underground army could not intimidate the country at large. The Muslim insurgents who battled against French suzerainty met with similar difficulties in the towns. The Algerian Arab quarters, with their attics and back alleys, provided excellent hiding places for urban guerrillas. Yet General Massu did gain almost complete success in clearing Algiers, even though the Algerians were as tough and ruthless as any guerrillas who ever handled a gun.

Terror, in other words, proved no substitute for victory. Back-alley killings may depress morale and weaken the waverers for a time. But terror must be transmuted into political power. As long as the people remain convinced that the government will win in the end, violence of the gangster type is apt to yield diminishing returns. Most men are optimists at heart. They believe that misfortune will strike someone else. Englishmen and Germans during World War II became accustomed to adapting their lives to air raids. Nowadays people accept traffic accidents as an inconvenience or as a misfortune, but certainly not as an unacceptable risk.

The use of bandit-like methods moreover can never endow its practitioners with the glamour that may be acquired in large-scale urban risings where the rebel banner waves over the barricades to inspire doubters and followers alike. Terrorists can, at best, levy illegal taxes by means of persuasion or political rackets. They may even succeed to some extent in setting up an armed lobby which for a time extorts concessions from a weak opponent. But sooner or later the terrorists must broaden the base of their support, must merge their struggle into a wider rising, or must pay the price for their miscalculations. Helicopters confer a tremendous advantage to the incumbent power in urban as well as in rural guerrilla fighting. Isolated quarters occupied by rebel forces can easily be deprived of water, electricity, and other essential services. They are liable to be surrounded, searched, and cleaned up piecemeal.

The successful guerrilla must be resigned to waging a long drawn-out war. In such a protracted struggle, much will depend on the combatants' will to win and on their ability to present a united front to the outside world. Western democratic countries intent on the suppression of a revolutionary campaign are subject to the contradictory pressures exercised by public opinion. Hence they have to be concerned over the peace-singer with her guitar as well as over the guerrilla with his Tommy gun. Partisans and counter-partisans alike must thus build up mass organizations to back their respective causes. Here, too, success breeds success. The people at large are swayed by the likelihood of victory as much as by hopes for a better world. Small, determined groups of fighters may be willing to throw away their lives in a magnificent gesture that aims for glory rather than victory. The great majority of men, however, are more prosaic in their calculations. Hence the Germans, for instance, had relatively little trouble with underground movements after their first great victories in 1940. Underground warfare only became serious when the *Endsieg* no longer seemed assured. Similarly, the revolt in Algeria began only after the French had given up in Indochina, and the uprising in Hungary followed the withdrawal of Soviet troops from neighboring Austria. For the same reason, successful anti-communist outbreaks are not to be expected in Eastern Europe at the present moment. The position might, however, well change if the Russian regime should weaken from within or become involved in a war against China.

Above all, counterguerrilla forces must convince their opponents that resistance is hopeless, that the guerrilla leadership is selfish, incompetent, corrupt, and divided, that surrender will bring neither dishonor, torture, nor death, and that capitulation is the only rational policy. This task is essential in the battle for the minds of the civilian population. The government forces should, at the same time, attempt to sow dissension among the enemy and should not disdain bribery where necessary. In the War of the Spanish Succession the merciless terror let loose upon the rebellious Camisards was of little avail to the king. The royalists made headway, however, when they began to use more politic methods. Jean Cavalier, the Camisards' most audacious leader, was won over by personal concessions and ended his career, by a strange combination of circumstances, as George II's Governor of Jersey and a British major-general.

Guerrillas and counterguerrillas alike, resembling hostile brothers, must be masters in the art of organizational infiltration. They must be trained to fight in the style of city gangsters, as mobile military units, as demolition squads, and as "pseudo gangs" in the countryside. Planned assassinations of key administrators and "prophylactic executions" of possible opponents now represent an important element of Viet Cong guerrilla strategy in Vietnam. This mode of warfare is not, of course, a communist invention. The *sicarius,* the Jewish Zealot who resorted to street-corner knifings to expel the Romans from Judea, was already a well-known problem to the occupation authorities who served the Caesars in the Holy Land. In the twentieth century, such killings have become a characteristic form of totalitarian warfare, of both the Nazi and the communist variety. The Chinese communists and their pupils have used all these techniques, and have incorporated them as an essential component of their guerrilla strategy. Planned murders, including preemptive liquidations, serve the three-fold purpose of removing potential leaders of the opposition, disrupting the enemy administration, and terrorizing the waverers. As the Viet Cong have shown, prophylactic assassination is a formidable weapon in the insurrectionary's armory.

The employment of terror against large numbers of medium-rank functionaries moreover seems to pay bigger dividends than assaults against a few highly placed men in the governmental hierarchy of the kind carried out by nineteenth-century anarchists. Nevertheless, terror has serious limitations. It may easily alienate public opinion. And, historically speaking, a strategy of assassination has never been successful on its own. Proponents of physical force among adherents of the "People's Will" group performed prodigious feats of ingenuity and courage in attacking high dignitaries of the tsarist regime. Yet these terrorists never managed to reach the Russian masses or to destroy the Russian monarchy. Subversion of the elitist kind reached even higher perfection among the Oriental sect known as Assassins which flourished many centuries earlier. The Assassins achieved an incredible degree of discipline and self-sacrifice among their adherents. Operating from well-secured bases, they carried out political murders with an astonishing degree of precision. Yet, lacking great armies or extensive guerrilla forces, they could effect nothing of permanent value.[55]

Guerrillas, like counterguerrillas, are lost, however, if they do not also have a constructive civilian program. The most effective partisans will look to the pursuits of peace as well as to those of war. They will act in the spirit of the ancient Jews

[55]The Assassins were adherents of the Ismaili doctrine of Islam. In 1090 Hasanibu-al-Sabbah seized the castle of Alamut, where he established his headquarters. He controlled an extensive network of agents and of trained terrorists who operated all over Persia and Iraq, subject to an extremely strict discipline. The Assassins struggled against the reigning Caliphate and, to a lesser extent, against the Caliphate of Cairo and the Christian Crusaders. The Assassins were extirpated in the thirteenth century by the invading Mongols.

86

mentioned in the book of Nehemiah, who rebuilt the walls of Jerusalem in the teeth of the enemy while, according to their leader, "half of my servants wrought in the work, and the other half held both the spears, the shields, and the bows and the habergeons."[56] Guerrillas and government forces alike need an effective civilian program. But the best programs are worthless, unless they can be effectively administered, and unless the administration is efficiently run. Guerrillas and counterguerrillas alike must therefore heed the lessons taught by colonial conquerors, such as Gallieni, that victory on the battlefield is useless without thorough-going governance of the civilian population. Effective administration, properly coordinated with military action, is indeed an essential condition of victory. The Viet Minh as well as the FLN displayed a sound understanding of this principle. So did the Irish, who built up an effective system of law courts while at the same time gunning down policemen of the Royal Irish Constabulary. No incumbent authority can win a guerrilla war, if it cannot outadminister and outpolice the enemy, and if it cannot provide effective protection to its subjects. Similarly, no guerrilla leader can effect a revolution if he cannot also govern, or if he remains a prisoner to the mindless revolutionary militarism that insists on the principle of "bomb now – rule later."

Sound government helps to win mass support. Mass support is vital; yet masses on their own can never win. Spontaneous risings like those which broke out against the communist régime in Eastern Germany stand little chance of success. Guerrillas require cadres. Even in the actual conduct of operations, quality counts for more than quantity; surprise and strategems may help to neutralize superior numbers. Modern guerrilla leaders in this respect can still learn from the military lessons embodied in the Old Testament. When Gideon, an outstanding Hebrew military chief, was preparing for battle against the Midianites, the Lord said to Gideon, "Now therefore go to, proclaim in the ears of the people, saying, Whosoever is fearful and afraid, let him return and depart early from Mount Gilead. And there returned of the people twenty and two thousand; and there remained ten thousand." From these Gideon, by a curious method of

[56] Nehemiah 4:16.

87

personnel selection, picked out three hundred chosen warriors. Gideon then "divided the three hundred men into three companies, and he put a trumpet into every man's hand, with empty pitchers, and lamps within the pitchers." The three commando companies then delivered a surprise attack on the enemy camp at night. "And the three companies blew the trumpets, and brake the pitchers, and held the lamps in their left hands and the trumpets in their right hands to blow withal: and they cried, The sword of the Lord and of Gideon. And they stood every man in his place round about the camp: and all the host ran, and cried and fled. And the three hundred blew the trumpets, and the Lord set every man's sword against his fellow, even throughout all the host: and the host fled to Beth-shittah in Zererath, and to the border of Abdel-meholah, unto Tabbath."[57]

The use of unconventional methods and of surprise may be applied on the psychological as well as on the tactical level. Guerrillas and counterguerrillas alike require a knowledge of the backgound and culture of the enemy in order to understand his thinking.

Guerrilla and counterguerrilla warfare alike can benefit, therefore, not merely from a mass basis but also from trained élite formations. Both partisan and anti-partisan warfare have become a highly specialized art. Military planners would thus do well to prepare "small wars" in advance. There is much to be said for developing unconventional forces as a permanent part of the existing armed forces. For guerrilla wars to some extent represent a regression to "limited" warfare. They also enable weaker powers to harry stronger states. The Egyptians thus were able to force the British out of the Suez Canal Zone. Yet the conflict over the evacuation of the Canal Zone might well have taken a different turn if the British had been able to rely on professional guerrilla units, operating in civilian clothes and capable of striking both within and outside the Canal Zone. In addition, however, guerrillas may have their part to play in conventional and even in nuclear warfare, for if atomic weapons are ever used on the battlefield, the enemy's rear may conceivably be the safest place for the defender's own forces.

[57] Judges 7:3, 16, 20, 21, 22.

At the same time, special emphasis must be given to the question of supply. Guerrillas depend on their ability to live off the land. They cannot afford big supply trains. They must be inured to austerity. If guerrillas learn this lesson, they will enjoy tremendous advantages over heavy, ponderous armies, slowed down by big administrative "tails." Yet partisans also require ammunition, food, and water. Though guerrillas may be disciplined into making do with simple food, their physiological needs are roughly the same as those of conventional soldiers. The image of the Asian guerrilla able to subsist forever on a handful of rice and a sip of water is as much of a mythological figure as the Indian trader who – in the imagination of many a white settler in Africa – can live "on the smell of an oil rag." Guerrillas can usually obtain food and clothing in their operational areas. But areas, ammunition, communication equipment, and medical supplies must either be captured or supplied by an outside power through underground channels.

The suppression of guerrillas thus depends to a very considerable extent on the ability of the occupying power to prevent supplies from falling into guerrilla hands. In Soviet-occupied Europe a centralized state machinery controls supplies effectively, and can therefore stifle guerrilla movements in disaffected areas. (In Malaya the British solved their problem by resettling villages in centralized locations that could be effectively protected. The British also instituted a stringent system of food rationing, and sometimes even central kitchens, thereby starving out the guerrillas.) This type of civilian support forms an essential complement to anti-partisan strategy. Counterguerrilla forces moreover must improve their own efficiency by adjusting their equipment to the areas of operation and by using helicopters for logistic as well as tactical purposes. The helicopter, in fact, promises to be the anti-guerrillas' maid-of-all-work. Unfortunately there are never enough of these air-borne trucks and gunboats.

Military action, however, should never be pursued for its own sake. Counterguerrilla warfare, like conventional wars, is politics by other means. Armed action must therefore correspond to its political objectives. "Butcher and bolt" actions are useless unless victories are consolidated by maneuvers designed to "clear and hold." The "clear and hold" strategy in turn must influence the way in which the enemy is assaulted on the battlefield. There is no point in attacks that inflict huge losses on the civilian population. Intelligence, preferably gathered by local agents, is worth more than the best equipment. Firepower can never be a substitute for brains. The most brilliant victories on the battlefield will avail little in the long run unless the enemy's underground political organization can be destroyed. The political cadres must be captured or killed; otherwise the enemy's armed formations can always return in good time. On its own, the strategy of "search and destroy" is likely to be as inadequate as eighteenth-century British tactics of riot control, which entailed waiting for an outbreak, calling out the Guards, firing into the mob, and marching the troops back to barracks until the next outbreak. As we have previously seen, the old police tactics of repression gave place in nineteenth-century England to the strategy of prevention. This in turn depended on the constable's doing his beat. Anti-guerrilla strategy likewise requires adequate prevention, which in turn hinges on the quality of the political and administrative personnel in the field.

Once an area has been cleared, civilian administrators must therefore immediately step in with resettlement and food supply programs, with publicity and – where necessary – with agricultural reform. The authorities must build up administrative cadres that are in touch with the people and that can gather intelligence, in order that military measures and civilian programs may complement one another. (In Malaya, for instance, British officials encouraged the supplying of information by promising complete anonymity for the informer. Ordinary people could mail unsigned letters about communist troop movements. Before sending off their letters, informers would tear off a strip at the edge. At the end of the emergency, they could claim the reward offered for information by matching their strip of paper against the document dispatched to the administration.) Information need not be extorted; information – like most other things – can be bought, provided always that the population is convinced that the war is going against the guerrillas and that governmental promises will be honored.

All these measures take time, and counterguerrilla opera-

90

tions are therefore an extraordinarily expensive kind of warfare for the suppressing forces. Partisans can choose the time and place of their attacks, while government forces have to defend the civilian population and also must wage war against the enemy. Over and over again, partisans have been able to pin down troops ten or twenty times their own strength. Providing that adequate forces are committed from the beginning, victory over a guerrilla force need not necessarily be too costly in terms of casualties. But with a policy of too-little-and-too-late or even barely-enough, such operations can exhaust the regular forces. The French never sent conscripts to Indochina, and by 1954 they were losing each year the equivalent of half the graduating class at St. Cyr, the French West Point. Similarly, the United States Regular Army in the thirty years following the Civil War lost a considerable portion of its strength in Indian wars. Guerrilla warfare can thus be extremely effective. Partisan operations have therefore captured the imagination of many nonmilitary intellectuals and have acquired an aura of invincibility.

Yet, when all is said and done, "small wars" remain the weapon of the weak, and history only stresses the lesson. Thus the Boers only resorted to guerrilla warfare in the South African War (1899-1902) after their main armies had been defeated in the field. The Yugoslavs only took to the mountains after their regular army had been swiftly crushed by the Germans in 1941. Guerrillas cannot win against a determined enemy unless they are supported by a foreign regular force (such as Wellington's expeditionary force in Spain), or unless they solve the difficult task of creating regular units of their own. Partisan tactics on their own can only succeed under certain circumstances. They need a secure source of supplies; the enemy must be disunited; his will to resist must be broken; or war must be waged over an issue which the incumbent power does not consider worth a protracted war. After prolonged fighting the French finally abandoned Algeria, even though their army remained un-defeated. But the French would never have abandoned Alsace-Lorraine, whatever the provocation, for they con-sidered Alsace an inalienable part of their national patrimony. The Israelis may consider guerrilla irruptions to be a serious threat, but they will never consent to liquidate their state for fear of partisans.

Regarding revolutions in general, nothing can be more dangerous to insurrectionary planners than the romantic notion that virtuous peoples – rightly struggling to be free – must necessarily win in their struggle against tyrants. This interpretation is based on a misconceived idea of revolutionary wars that many textbooks still help to perpetuate. According to the old version, the Americans won the War of Independence because the British Redcoats were no match against liberty-loving farmers sniping from behind cover against the over-disciplined regulars. The French revolutionary forces are said to have been invincible because the revolutionaries alone were able to enforce conscription and to develop the tactics of the massed column. But the American War of Independence was not mainly won by guerrillas but by regular soldiers and sailors. British soldiers were perfectly capable of becoming as skilled in skirmishing as their American opponents. The French revolutionary generals merely perfected methods of impressment already used by Louis XIV in the War of the Spanish Succession and by Gustavus Adolphus in the Thirty Years' War. French revolutionary tacticians drew heavily on the work of military theoreticians of the later Bourbon period, just as revolutionary civilian administrators continued and perfected the work accomplished by the statesmen of the *ancien régime.*

Many revolutions moreover have come to grief. The German Spartakists (later known as Communists) could not seize power after World War I. Many nationalities never succeeded in creating independent states of their own. The Basques, Georgians, Catalonians, and Flemings are not likely ever to achieve representation in the United Nations as sovereign states. There is nothing inevitable about revolutionary success. Besides, many of the most successful revolutionaries would have failed but for foreign aid. Neither the Yugoslav partisans nor the Chinese communists, for instance, could win by their own efforts alone. Without British help, Tito could hardly have survived during World War II. When his forces finally entered Belgrade, he also had the indispensable support of the Soviet Army. The Long March of the Chinese communists in the 1930s was a long flight. Had Chiang Kai-shek, in 1937, been able to use his best units against the communists rather than the Japanese,

Mao Tse-tung today might well be living as an exile in Moscow.

Military planners in the past have often made the mistake of underestimating the guerrilla. The danger now exists that the pendulum may swing too far the other way, and that partisan warfare will be overrated and come to be looked upon as a military panacea. Truth, however, lies with neither extreme; "revolutionary wars" fought by guerrilla actions still remain only one of many forms of human conflict.

A Selected Bibliography

Abd-el-Krim. *Memoiren: Mein Krieg gegen Spanien und Frankreich.* Dresden, C. Reissner, 1927.

Alderson, E. A. H. *With the Mounted Infantry and Mashonaland Field Force, 1896.* London, Methuen and Co., 1898.

American University, Washington, D.C. Special Operations Research Office. *Case Studies in Insurgency and Revolutionary Warfare.* 4 vols. Washington, D.C., 1963-1964.

_____. Special Operations Research Office. *A Counterinsurgency Bibliography.* By D. M. Condit [*et al.*]. Washington, D.C., 1963.

Amery, L. S., ed. *The Times History of the War in South Africa 1899-1902.* 7 vols. London, Sampson, Low, Marston and Co., 1900-1909.

Arias, Juan de Dios. *Reseña histórica de la formación y operaciones del cuerpo de Ejército del Norte durante la intervención francesa....* Mexico, N. Chavez, 1867.

Bennett, Richard. *The Black and Tans.* London, Edward Hulton, 1959.

Bode, Colonel — . *Abd el Krim's Freiheitskampf gegen Franzosen und Spanier.* Berlin, Verlag Offene Worte, 1926.

Churchill, Winston S. *Marlborough: His Life and Times.* 6 vols. New York, Charles Scribner's Sons, 1933-1938.

Clausewitz, Karl von. *On War.* Trans. J. J. Graham. New and rev. ed. with introd. and notes by F. N. Maude.... 3 vols. London, Kegan Paul, Trench, Trubner and Co., 1940.

94

Craig, Gordon Alexander. *The Battle of Koniggratz Prussia's Victory over Austria, 1866.* Philadelphia, J. B. Lippincott, 1964.

Crozier, Brian. *The Rebels: A Study of Post-War Insurrections.* London, Chatto and Windus, 1960.

Delbrück, Hans. *Geshichte der Kriegskunst im Rahmen der politischen Geschichte.* Photomechanical reproduction of the 3rd ed. With an introd. by Karl Christ. Berlin, W. de Gruyter, 1964–.

Dixon, C. Aubrey, and Otto Heilbrunn. *Communist Guerrilla Warfare.* With a foreword by Sir Reginald F. S. Denning. New York, Frederick A. Praeger, 1954.

Dziewanowski, M. K. *Joseph Pilsudski: A European Federalist, 1918-1922.* Stanford, Calif., Hoover Institution Press, 1969.

Earle, Edward Mead., *et al.,* eds. *Makers of Modern Strategy: Military Thought from Machiavelli to Hitler.* New York, Atheneum, 1966.

Emerit, Marcel. *L'Algérie à l'époque d'Abd-el-Kader.* Paris, Editions Larose, 1951.

Engels, Friedrich. *Der deutsche Bauernkrieg.* Berlin, Verlag Neuer Weg. 1946.

_____. ''Neue Bedingungen des bewaffneten Aufstandes'' in *F. Engels and V. I. Lenin, Militärpolitische Schriften,* K. Schmidt, ed. Berlin, Internationaler Arbeiter-Verlag, 1930.

Falls, Cyril Bentham. *The Art of War: From the Age of Napoleon to the Present Day.* London and New York, Oxford University Press, 1961.

Franz, Günther. *Der deutsche Bauernkrieg.* 2 vols. Munich and Berlin, R. Oldenbourg, 1933-1935.

Freytag-Loringhoven, H. F. P., Freiherr von. *Die Psyche der Heere*. Berlin, Mittler und Sohn, 1923.

Friedjung, Heinrich. *Der Kampf um die Vorherrschaft in Deutschland, 1859 bis 1866*. 2 vols. Berlin, J. G. Cotta, 1912.

Galula, David. *Counterinsurgency Warfare; Theory and Practice*. New York, Frederick A. Praeger, 1964.

Gann, L. H. "The Development of Southern Rhodesia's Military System, 1890-1953," National Archives of Rhodesia, *Occasional Papers*, No. 1, 1965.

──────────. *A History of Southern Rhodesia: Early Days to 1934*. London, Chatto and Windus, 1965.

Giraldus Cambrensis. *The Itinerary through Wales* and *The Description of Wales*. Introd. by W. Llewlyn Williams. London, J. M. Dent, 1908.

Guedalla, Philip. *The Two Marshals: Bazaine, Pétain*. New York, Reynal and Hitchcock, 1943.

Guevara, Ernesto. *Che Guevara on Guerrilla Warfare*. With an introd. by Harries-Clichy Peterson. New York, Frederick A. Praeger, 1961.

Heilbrunn, Otto. *Partisan Warfare*. With a foreword by C. M. Woodhouse. New York, Frederick A. Praeger, 1962.

──────────. *Warfare in the Enemy's Rear*. With a foreword by Sir John Winthrop Hackett. London, George Allen and Unwin, 1963.

Henderson, Ian, with Philip Goodhart. *Manhunt in Kenya*. Garden City, N.Y., Doubleday and Co., 1958.

Herd, Norman. *1922: The Revolt on the Rand*. Johannesburg, Blue Crane Books, 1966.

Hobsbawm, Eric J. *Primitive Rebels: Studies in Archaic Forms of Social Movements in the 19th and 20th Centuries.* Manchester University Press, 1959.

Hobson, John Atkinson. *Imperialism: A Study.* London, George Allen and Unwin, 1902.

Howe, Samuel Gridley. *An Historical Sketch of the Greek Revolution.* Rev. ed. with an introd. and notes by George Georgiades Arnakis. Austin, Texas, Center for Neo-Hellenic Studies, 1966.

James, C. L. R. *The Black Jacobins: Toussaint L'Ouverture and the San Domingo Revolution.* 2nd ed., rev. New York, Vintage Books, 1963.

Kühnrich, Heinz. *Der Partisanenkrieg in Europa 1939-1945.* 2nd rev. ed. Berlin, Dietz, 1968.

Lawrence, T. E. "Guerrilla," in *Encyclopaedia Britannica,* Vol. X. London, 14th ed., 1929.

_____. *Seven Pillars of Wisdom, a Triumph.* London, J. Cape, 1935.

Leighton, Richard M., and Ralph Sanders, ed. *Insurgency and Counterinsurgency: An Anthology.* Washington, D.C., Industrial College of the Armed Forces, October 1962. (Publication No. R-226)

Lenin, V. I. "Der Partisanenkrieg," in F. Engels and V. I. Lenin, *Militärpolitische Schriften.* K. Schmidt, ed. Berlin, Internationaler Arbeiter-Verlag, 1930.

Macardle, Dorothy. *The Irish Republic: A Documented Chronicle of the Anglo-Irish Conflict and the Partitioning of Ireland, with a Detailed Account of the Period 1916-1923.* London, Victor Gollancz, 1937.

Macaulay, Thomas Babington. *The History of England from the Accession of James II.* Chicago, Bedford and Clarke, 1888.

Mao Tse-tung. *On Guerrilla Warfare.* Trans. Samuel B. Griffith. New York, Frederick A. Praeger, 1961.

Marx, Karl. *Revolution und Kontre-Revolution in Deutschland.* Stuttgart, T. H. W. Dietz Nachf., 1920.

Maurice, J. F. *Hostilities Without Declaration of War: An Historical Abstract of the Cases in which Hostilities Have Occurred Between Civilized Powers Prior to Declaration of War or Warning. From 1700 to 1870.* London, H. M. Stationery Office, 1883.

Mosley, Leonard Oswald. *Gideon Goes to War.* New York, Scribner's, 1955.

Niox, Gustave Léon. *Expédition du Mexique, 1861-1867: Récit Politique et Militaire.* Paris, J. Dumaine, 1874.

Osanka, Franklin Mark, ed. *Modern Guerrilla Warfare: Fighting Communist Guerrilla Movements, 1941-1961.* Introd. by Samuel P. Huntington. New York, Free Press of Glencoe, 1962.

Palmer, R. R. *The Age of Democratic Revolution: A Political History of Europe and America, 1760-1800: The Struggle.* Princeton University Press, 1964.

Paret, Peter, and John W. Shy. *Guerrillas in the 1960's.* New York, Frederick A. Praeger, 1962.

Pringle, Patrick, *Hue and Cry: The Birth of the British Police Force.* London, Museum Press, 1955.

Reith, Sir Charles. *A New Study of Police History.* Edinburgh, Oliver and Boyd, 1956.

Ross, Sir William David, ed. *The Student's Oxford Aristotle . . . Politics and Poetics.* London, Oxford University Press, 1942.

Rousset, Camille. *La Conquête de l'Algérie 1841-1857.* 2 vols. Paris, Librairie Plon, 1904.

Seton Watson, Hugh. *Eastern Europe Between the Wars 1918-1941.* 3rd rev. ed. New York, Harper and Row, 1962.

Stewart, A. T. Q. *The Ulster Crisis.* London, Faber and Faber, 1967.

Thompson, Robert. *No Exit from Vietnam.* New York, David McKay Company, 1969.

Valeriano, Napoleon D., and Charles T. R. Bohannan. *Counter-Guerrilla Operations: the Philippine Experience.* New York, Frederick A. Praeger, 1962.

Volbach, W. F. *Mainz.* Berlin, Deutscher Kunstverlag, 1928.

Wilson, R. D. *Cordon and Search, with 6th Airborne Division in Palestine.* Aldershot [Eng.], Gale and Polden, 1949.